Athletes' Guide to MENTAL TRAINING

Robert M. Nideffer, PhD

President, Enhanced Performance Associates, San Diego

FEB

Human Kinetics Publishers, Inc.
Champaign, Illinois

Library of Congress Cataloging in Publication Data

Nideffer, Robert M.
    Athletes' guide to mental training.

    Bibliography: p.
    Includes index.
    1. Sports—Psychological aspects. 2. Physical
education and training—Psychological aspects.
3. Attention. 4. Stress (Psychology). I. Title.
GV706.4.N49   1985   796'.01   85-4395
ISBN 0-931250-96-X

Production Director: Sara Chilton
Typesetter: Yvonne Sergent
Text Layout: Janet Davenport
Cover Design: Janet Davenport
Cover Photograph: Wilmer Zehr
Printed by: Phillips Brothers Printers

ISBN: 0-931250-96-X
Copyright © by Robert M. Nideffer

Printed in the United States of America

10 9 8 7 6 5 4 3 2 1

Human Kinetics Publishers, Inc.
Box 5076 • Champaign, IL 61820

Preface

The Sports Medicine Committee of the USOC voted to fund the Elite Athlete Development Project as part of the preparation for the 1984 Olympic Games in Los Angeles. This project sought to provide current information in the sport sciences to athletes and coaches who were likely to be involved in the 1984 Olympic Games. Track and field, weight lifting, cycling, fencing, and volleyball were the five sports that initially participated in this pilot project. Experts in biomechanics, sport psychology, exercise physiology, and nutrition were identified and asked to volunteer their time to work with coaches and athletes in these sports. It was through this Elite Athlete Development Project that pyschologists like myself were given the opportunity to work with U.S. Olympic level athletes and coaches. I was able to work with coaches and athletes in training camps and at various competitions throughout the 1980-84 quadrenium.

A major logistical problem I encountered in providing psychological services was finding a way to maintain continuity and provide follow-up services. For example, when working with the men's track and field team, I often found that the coaches and athletes were almost entirely different from one meet to the next. In fact, only about 20% of the athletes who participated in the 1983 World Championships in Helsinki made the 1984 U.S. Olympic Team! The number of athletes to be served, the geographical distances to be covered, and the limited resources (e.g., availability of other sport psychologists to provide follow-up services) meant that some type of training program and resource materials were needed. Somehow, both coaches and athletes had to learn how to be their own "sport psychologists."

In response to the demands of the competitive situations our athletes faced, I developed a structured psychological training program which could be used by all athletes, regardless of sport. It contains testing programs to help provide a specific training focus with individual athletes and audio tapes to facilitate mental rehearsal and to assist individuals in controlling both concentration and arousal.

An evaluation of this sport psychology program following the Olympic Games indicated that although the program had been a success, sport psychologists had still much to do. We needed to expand the education that had begun at an elite level across all sports at all levels. We also needed to improve the delivery system in order to put this information into the hands of those who most needed it. In *Athletes' Guide to mental Training*, I present this psychological training program developed for our Olympic Athletes. It is one way to disseminate this information more widely to athletes and coaches who compete at all levels, from high school through the professional ranks.

I begin the book by providing you with an understanding of the critical roles that both concentration (what you pay attention to) and physical arousal (how much muscle tension you develop) play in determining your level of performance. Several different ways to concentrate during competition are then explained. Next you will learn that a key to successful performance involves being able to shift from one type of concentration to another at precisely the right time.

You also will learn to identify the different types of concentration necessary in your sport. Then, you will learn to use special psychological techniques such as mental rehearsal, relaxation training, centering techniques, and attention control training to help you maintain control over both concentration and arousal.

For those individuals who are using psychological techniques for the first time, a general training program is provided at the end of the book. This program provides a structured way for the novice to begin applying the procedures presented.

Over the past few years, the methods presented in this book have been applied in virtually every major sporting country in the world. The procedures of mental rehearsal, centering, and attention control training have been used in both team sports (e.g., basketball, baseball, soccer, football, hockey, and volleyball) and individual sports (e.g., skating, diving, swimming, gymnastics, archery, shooting, judo, cycling, golf, tennis, fencing, weight lifting and track and field). Sport psychology contributed substantially to our efforts in the 1984 Olympics, and I am confident it will contribute even more in future years as our psychological training programs become even better.

It is with a great deal of gratitude that I thank members of the USOC Sports Medicine Council for their support of the Elite Athlete Development Project, especially Dr. Irving Dardick, Dr. Casey Clarke, Dr. Harmon Brown, and Dr. Paul Ward. Thanks, too, to some of the other sport psychologists involved, specifically, Dr. Betty Wenz, Dr. Richard Suinn, Dr. William Morgan, Dr. Bruce Ogilvie, and Dr. Rainer Martens. I also would like to thank Basketball Canada and U.S. Diving for their involvement. Special thanks go to Dr. Cal Botterill, Jack Donohue, Ron O'Brien, and Dennis Golden. Lastly, and most importantly, thanks to the athletes who supported this work through their efforts.

Contents

1

"The Thrill of Victory and the Agony of Defeat"

Although it happened back in 1966, the experience was so intense it could have been yesterday. I was warming up on the 1 meter board prior to an intercollegiate meet. It was "just another meet," so I wasn't feeling anything special. A fair-sized crowd was watching as we were diving indoors. For my first dive, I had decided to do a reverse layout with a half-twist. Feeling relaxed, this was a dive I normally enjoyed. It involved taking the normal front dive approach, and then, after lifting off the board, reversing direction and diving headfirst in a back dive position, back toward the diving board. At the very top of the dive, I would add a half-twist by dropping one shoulder, and turning my head to look back and down toward the diving board, then enter the water headfirst in the same position as if I had done an inward dive.

My approach toward the end of the diving board was uneventful; I wasn't aware of anything special until my hurdle step. As I came back down on the board however, I could feel the board bending beneath me. Suddenly as the board reached the bottom of its downward bend and snapped back up, something also snapped inside of me.

In that fraction of a second where the transition of movement (from moving downward to being catapulted into the air) occurred, I knew instantly that the dive would be perfect. I was in total control, knowing what would happen before it actually happened without consciously having to do anything. It was as if my body was on automatic pilot, and the pilot was perfect.

1

As the board sprung back up, catapulting me into the air, time slowed down. I seemed to sail up forever, feeling at the very top of the dive like I was hanging effortlessly in midair, and smiling uncontrollably in response. I knew that when I came down, I would be very close to the diving board. I could feel exactly where I was in the air, and even though I couldn't see the diving board, I knew that I would miss it, but not by more than a couple of inches.

While I was enjoying my suspension in midair, I heard several people in the crowd scream. I knew they thought I was going to land on my head on the diving board. Smiling smugly with my secret, I was the only one there who knew that I would miss the board—I was in total control!

At the very top of the dive, I dropped my right shoulder, twisted, and began descending toward the diving board. As I turned in the air, with seemingly all the time in the world, I could see and examine the faces in the crowd: Frightened, some were staring with mouths open; some had hands in front of their eyes, trying not to see me "kill myself"; and others seemed to be eagerly anticipating my disaster.

As I missed the board by about 2 inches and entered the water without a ripple, my feeling of exhilaration was complete. I had just performed the best dive of my life! For a moment, time had stood still, and I knew what it was like to have total concentration and total control.

One week later, however, the "thrill of victory" turned into "the agony of defeat" in a meet at Oregon State. There I experienced the opposite of total control. Once again, I was diving 1 meter indoors. I remember being more anxious about this meet for two reasons: Oregon State had a couple of good divers, and I would be diving off a new kind of board for the first time. I had always dived off aluminum boards, but Oregon State had a new type of metal board that was much slower. With the aluminum boards, the time it took for the board to bend down and then rebound was very quick. With the board at Oregon State, I felt like I was on a trampoline, having to wait for the board to catapult me into the air. I was like the pole vaulter who has used a metal pole all his life: He shows up at a meet and finds he has to use a fiberglass pole.

Because we were diving in a dual meet, the judges selected prior to the start of the competition a required dive which each diver had to execute. The dive selected was a reverse dive and I chose to perform it in a pike position. My anxiety was increased when I found out that I would be the first diver. I always disliked being first because the judges have not established a standard for comparison yet. As a result, their evaluations vary a great deal and the first diver is frequently scored lower.

To do the reverse dive correctly, I had to make my normal front approach and then, as I lifted off the board, pull my feet up over my head. My hands and feet would come together in an inverted "jackknife" position at the top of the dive. From that position I would drop my head and shoulders back toward the board and enter the water headfirst.

One of my opponents, sensing my nervousness, managed to make things worse in an obvious, yet successful attempt to "psych me out." He waited until I was walking to the diving board and then stepped in front of me asking me to wait a minute. He walked over to the scoring table and, in a voice loud enough for me to hear, complained that the end of the diving board was slippery. The referee held me up long enough to check the board. Although I knew the board wasn't slippery, as I began my hurdle step I remember thinking "don't slip."

Well, I didn't slip, but with my concentration on the board and my increased muscle tension, I failed to wait for the board to catapult me upward. I leaned out too soon, causing the board to catapult me out instead of up. As I pulled my feet up and reached out to touch my toes, I did a sit-up instead of bringing my feet all the way up to the ceiling. Then, as I dropped my shoulders, I looked for the water, but I could not see it! With a sinking feeling in my stomach I rolled my head slightly to one side and I saw the people sitting in the balcony. I was parallel to the pool surface. I was stuck in midair, balanced and unable to do anything to save the dive. All I could do was grit my teeth and wait for the inevitable pain from landing flat on my back.

That dive seemed to set the tone for the rest of the meet. I never recovered, and things went from bad to worse. I remember leaving Oregon State with the lowest point total I had received in 2 years. Like the San Diego Charger football team and their magnificent victory over the Miami

Dolphins in the 1982 playoffs, only to be destroyed by the Cincinnati Bengals the next week, I had gone from total control to total disaster in just 7 days.

2

"Mind Like Water"—Total Concentration 1

Talk with other athletes, or read about some of their experiences and you will find that the type of experience I described in Chapter 1 is not unusual in sport. Basketball players will remember times when they were totally aware of the basketball court, and everything just seemed to flow. They felt loose and relaxed and movement was effortless. Like Dr. J., they could jump and hang suspended in the air, retaining total control over their bodies. If they took a shot at the basket, they knew even before the ball left their hand that it was going in.

John Brodie, a former quarterback with the San Francisco 49ers, talks about similar experiences in professional football. He remembers dropping back for a pass and seeing the whole field. In an instant he had become aware of the future: He would throw the ball before the receiver had made his cut, and yet he would know that the defender would be beaten, and that the ball would be caught; he could anticipate the exact position of the receiver and the defenders as they raced to the ball; then, he could sit back and watch his own pass seem to sail out in slow motion as the drama he predicted would unfold.

The experience of knowing what will happen, of slowing things down, and of having them appear bigger than they really are, occurs in many sports. Baseball players will have days when they see the ball much better. They seem to be able to slow it down, watching the rotation as it approaches the plate.

Some will even maintain that they can watch the ball make contact with the bat.

I have talked with skeet shooters who tell me with great enthusiasm about the day they "couldn't miss"!

> I felt extremely confident as I was standing on the station. We had both gone straight (not missed) for 250 targets. He was shooting extremely well, but I knew I would win. We went through another 150 targets before he finally missed. What a day! The targets seemed as big as dinner plates and so slow! I never had to scratch and claw—I was on! If I could just do that all the time!

"If I could just do that all the time!" Although such total concentration is not that unusual in sport, it is not that usual either. "If we could just do it all the time!" In this book you will learn why it doesn't happen all the time and how to increase the probability of it happening more often.

In the early 1960s, Bud Winter, the San Jose State University track coach, discovered one of the difficulties which kept his athletes from achieving total concentration. Winter's sprinters would come to the track and, seemingly without trying, would run near world record times in practice. Often, they would be amazed by their own performance and would vow that the next time they ran they would break the world record. "If it was this easy, I shouldn't have any problem!" More often than not, to their own great disappointment, they would run slower the second time. They would try too hard, tightening up and working against themselves. Winter sought to alleviate the problem by asking these sprinters to run at 80-90% of their maximum effort. This simple change in thought process (e.g., thinking about 80% instead of 100%) would keep them from tightening up.

When you are experiencing this kind of flow or concentration, you are not working. You are not "scratching and clawing" or giving it 110%. It is not that you are not motivated or do not care; in fact, nothing could be farther from the truth. Instead, you have gotten so much into the immediacy of the experience that you are simply allowing things to happen. Your attention is directed externally to the things going on around you almost to the exclusion of any internal, analytical thinking. You are reacting so automatically that you do not have to consciously direct your body; you are simply letting it do what it has been trained to do. When everything is "right," there is no self-criticism, no adjustment, no need for a director or an analyzer.

Masters of karate and aikido refer to the special state of concentration where everything occurs automatically as "making your mind like the water." When you are in complete control of your mind, you are able to keep your own anxiety as well as external distractors from interfering with concentration. Your mind is like the surface of a still pond, reflecting a mirror image of its surroundings. If the surroundings change, so does the mirror image.

To be ready to respond to an attack by any, or all of the people around him, the aikido expert must not focus attention on any one individual for any length of time. If he allows himself to concentrate on one person, he will quickly lose awareness of the others and of his surroundings. He is no longer reflecting a mirror image. By the same token, if he lets his attention become focused inside his own head, getting caught up in his own thoughts and feelings, he will lose awareness and become vulnerable. Each consciously directed thought (each subvocalization or comment you make to yourself) represents a momentary distractor and disturbs the "mirror image." Although conscious thoughts will help the aikido instructor to recreate memories of this situation later (should he survive), they are also likely to interfere with his performance. Thus, by avoiding these thoughts and by not concentrating on any one thing for too long, he is maintaining a "mind like water" and is retaining his ability to react quickly to sudden changes or to an attack.

If the sport you play is so well learned that you can perform automatically, it is possible to achieve the kind of flowing experience described earlier. In this instance, even in response to an attack, conscious thought is not required in order to perform, and attention does not have to be narrowed, nor does it need to be directed internally.

SUMMARY

Chapter 2 introduces the special state of concentration in which everything occurs automatically. Masters of karate and aikido refer to it as "making your mind like water." During performance of their sport, many athletes have the occasional wonderful experience when they feel everything just flows, and they are in total control without conscious effort.

It is possible to *make* such moments happen if you keep the following points in mind:

1. This total concentration requires a freedom from internal distractions.

2. The "mind like water" or flow experience requires performance skills so well learned that they can be done automatically.

3. Excessive anxiety or tension from trying too hard are primary factors preventing the development of a broad external type of concentration. Fear or the attempt to give 110% breaks this total focus of attention.

Subsequent chapters will outline the specific things that can be done to increase the frequency of such flowing "mind like water" experiences.

3

"The Focus of Ki"—Total Concentration 2

The "focus of ki" is in marked contrast to the type of total concentration described in chapter 2. Occasionally, athletes will describe an experience in which concentration was so narrowly focused, and so total, that they have no memory of the actual experience. I remember John Powell, a former world record holder in the discus, and Tom Petranoff, a world record holder in the javelin, both saying they could not remember what went on during their world record throws. They remember stepping into the ring (discus) or moving to the starting point. In Tom's case, he also remembers the end of the throw. "I remember noticing or thinking that my pull was incredibly long. But I can't remember anything else." It's an intense concentration that begins to explain the loss of memory. When watching John Powell compete it is easy to see why other competitors describe him as intense and tough. At one particular competition, he was by far the lightest of the throwers, and if body weight counted at all, he should not have been in the competition, yet he won.

Watching the eyes of the contestants as they moved across the ring, I could actually see most of them "mentally" working to make adjustments. It was obvious that conscious thought was going on during the throw. The athletes were monitoring their own performance and giving themselves instructions. Powell was an exception. His eyes didn't seem to indicate any active monitoring of what was going on. Once he initiated his throw, he was "on automatic." I had the feeling if someone had suddenly constructed a brick wall in front of the discus ring, it would not have altered Powell's throw or his follow-through. He would have been oblivious to the change because his concentration was so intense and so focused.

John Powell was the image of what my aikido instructors had referred to as "focusing ki." As practitioners of the martial arts, we had been told that at times our concentration would have to be completely focused. For the integration of mind and body, all mental and physical energy must flow in the same direction. For John Powell to get maximum effort into a discus throw, he would have to narrow his concentration. Making his "mind like water," developing that broad focus of attention, would not lead to the focus of strength he would need at the time of release in throwing the discus.

My aikido instructor was remarkable in his ability to shift easily from one type of concentration to another. One minute he would be flowing, moving effortlessly, aware of everything going on around him. If we were attacking him at this time, we were overcome as much by our own movement as by his. His throws did not require great strength; they simply required timing. Like the talented offensive lineman in football who meets the charge of the defensive lineman and then uses the momentum of that charge against the defense, so, too, would my instructor use our momentum against us. Then, suddenly, my instructor would shift his concentration and execute a technique requiring more intense or focused concentration. If he had to meet strength with strength, or if he was trying to move through an object or to break several boards or bricks, he would "focus his ki."

When tennis players or baseball hitters talk about "getting into the zone" or about shutting out everything but the ball, they have succeeded in focusing their ki. When world class throwers talk about "hitting the hole in the sky," they, too, have successfully focused their ki.

Obviously, a great many sport situations require this focused concentration, yet this type of total concentration seldom occurs. In fact, it happens so rarely, few of us really know what we are capable of. When we find out, the results are often astounding!

Prior to the 1983 Pepsi track meet in which he set a world

record of 327 feet in the Javelin, Tom Petranoff's longest competitive throw had been under 300 feet. Approximately 2 weeks before the Pepsi meet, I received a telephone call from Tom. He had read an article I had written describing the importance of concentration and control over physical tension and was convinced that "mental control" was keeping him from throwing the javelin 330 feet. He knew he was physically strong enough to throw that distance and he knew he had the technical skill. In Tom's mind, it was simply a matter of "putting it all together."

The biomechanical and motor aspects of throwing the javelin had long become "automatic" for Tom, but he was still having difficulty with controlling his concentration and his own tendency to try too hard. He indicated he was having difficulty shutting off the "self-talk" just prior to beginning his throw. He would stand at the head of the runway, and instead of concentrating on his approach, he would be distracted by noises, by the crowd, by his own instructions, and sometimes by frustration.

In addition to these concentration disturbances that interfered with the "focus of ki," Tom would try too hard and tense up just like Bud Winter's sprinters. The excessive muscle tension in his shoulder, arm, and hand would interfere with the release of the javelin and with his achieving maximum extension. When the javelin is gripped too tightly, it wobbles when released and distance is decreased. The goal for a thrower is to hold the javelin "like a captive bird," neither so hard he crushes it, nor so loose that it escapes.

To begin to develop control over concentration and muscle tension, Tom began practicing the psychological skills which I describe in this book. He used the centering procedure described in chapter 9 to control his breathing. Standing at the head of the runway, Tom picked out a spot on the ground about 2 feet in front of him. He stared at the spot and at the same time inhaled deeply from his abdomen, and then exhaled slowly. On the exhale, he consciously thought about relaxing his right arm and shoulder. The spot at which he was staring began to blur and his attention became focused on his own heartbeat. By relaxing and shutting out external distractors (the crowd), Tom was able to monitor his own arousal by feeling his pounding heart which became his signal: It told him when he was ready. By centering and by directing his attention to control muscle tension and mental distractions, Tom had achieved a state of focused concentration. His own positive interpretation of his beating heart ("As I feel my heartbeat picking up, I know that I'm ready.") not only signaled him when to go, but added to his confidence.

As a result of his physical training and his new mental training, Tom went into the Pepsi meet fully prepared. Prior to that meet, the world record was 317 feet, a record that had stood for over 10 years. Tom not only broke it, he shattered it, throwing the javelin over 327 feet!

The picture (Figure 3.1) of Tom Petranoff, throwing the javelin in a meet against the East Germans in Los Angeles, dramatically illustrates the integration of mind and body, and the focus of ki. Obviously, it takes a great deal of strength to throw the javelin over 300 feet. By looking at the expression on Tom's face, it is easy to see that his thoughts are focused on one thing—that "hole in the sky" he wants to send the javelin through. He does not have the kind of glassy stare we see when someone is daydreaming or unduly stressed; nor does he have the type of gaze we associate with deep thought or active problem solving. Instead, he has the fixed gaze associated with an intensely narrow type of concentration.

You can also see in Figure 3.1 the success Tom had in getting control over excessive muscle tension, especially the muscle tension antagonistic to his throw. Look at the relaxation in Tom's left hand, the one not holding the javelin. Then, too, look at his right hand. The javelin truly is being held like "a captive bird." Those muscles which need to be relaxed are, and those which need to contract maximally are prepared to do so. Somehow, Tom has differentiated levels of tension in his body and, as a result, he is not working against himself. He is not trying too hard, everything is working together, mind and body are one, and the results are obvious.

What would you be capable of achieving if you could "focus your ki" and develop that narrow type of concentration? How far could you drive a golf ball? How fast could you hit a serve in tennis if you had optimal control over muscle tension and if you were not working against yourself?

FIGURE 3.1 Tom Petranoff's 327-foot javelin throw illustrates the "focus of Ki." (Mickey Pfleger, *Sports Illustrated*, reproduced by permission)

SUMMARY

Chapter 3 introduces a very narrow type of total concentration. Masters of the martial arts refer to it as "the focus of ki." In order to use it effectively in a competitive sport situation, you must keep the following points in mind:

1. A narrow focus of concentration is required when strength and intensity are critical determinants of optimal performance (e.g., hitting a ball, throwing for distance, etc.).

2. The "focus of ki," like the development of a broad type of concentration, requires freedom from the mental distractors that act to increase muscle tension in those muscles that are antagonistic to performance.

The following chapter will discuss three keys to learning a narrow focus of total concentration and to performing at your optimal level.

4

Keys to Total Concentration

Developing control over your concentration is the only way to discover your real capabilities. You will then perform much closer to your own optimal level. To do this, you must be willing to spend time training your mind as well as your body. Highly skilled and experienced athletes know that great performances are as much mental as physical. If that is true, why then do more athletes not spend time developing their mental skills?

Some of the keys you can use to unlock your ability to concentrate, to "make your mind like water," and to be able to "focus your ki" will be discussed in this chapter.

Attention to self-instructions during performance splits concentration and prevents the integration of mind and body. Obviously, if you have to think about a skill while doing it, you will not be able to achieve the same high level of competence possible with automatic performance. Thinking can be very disruptive to performance! Just ask divers, gymnasts, or high jumpers if they inhale on take-off or hold their breath! A prerequisite to optimal performance is your having developed a skill to the point where it is possible to execute it automatically.

Many athletes often perform far below their capabilities because they are not able to shut off the announcer inside the head.

Learning a new skill requires a great deal of self-analysis. You need to have that voice in your head telling you what to do, commenting on the things you are doing, and patting you on the back when you do them correctly. Once you have learned the skill, however, that little voice needs to be silenced. As you will notice with the commentators on television, a running commentary tends to continue long after the actual event has occurred. If a football play would take as long to develop as it does to describe, a game could last all day!

Look at the picture of Dave McKenzie (Figure 4.1) throwing the hammer, and you may be able to get a feel for some of the problems that develop when you think too much about performance! Dave's head position suggests that mentally he is following the hammer, kind of talking to it as he is trying to throw. Although this is probably not actually happening with Dave, when it does occur, the talk that is going on inside his head interferes. In Dave's case, the conversation might sound something like this: "Okay, I can feel the pull. It feels as if my back is a little out of position. I've got to straighten out or I'll lose control over the hammer. Oops, I need more of an angle for release! Come on now. Hard!" If this kind of dialogue

FIGURE 4.1 Dave McKenzie, one of America's finest hammer throwers, in action. (Duomo Photography, reproduced by permission)

were going on, the hammer would be throwing Dave. In effect, he would be waiting for feedback from the 16 pound ball to tell him what to do next. In this case, both his thoughts and his body would always be just a little behind. With timing slightly off, he would be trying to catch up. It would be almost impossible to get everything into the throw. With the hammer out in front, as he tried to give a complete effort at the end, he would feel as if he had never really gotten his weight into the throw. The resistance that he would feel when he gets everything into the throw just would not be there. The hammer would be gone before he could catch up and get all of his weight behind it.

Wayne Gretsky, the hockey player, is a good example of an athlete who has practiced his moves until they are reflexive and, in doing so, has been able to quiet the little voice inside of him. His ability to respond to the play, to be where the puck is, to anticipate where other players will be on the ice, and to react quickly and seemingly "instinctively" sets him apart from other hockey players. Many hockey players are stronger, faster, quicker, have better shots, or are better skaters. Few, however, have the anticipation and awareness of everything that is taking place on the ice that Gretsky has. Because of this, people tend to see Wayne Gretsky as especially gifted, yet Gretsky says, "some people forget how much time I've spent developing my hockey skills."

Wayne Gretsky has paid his dues. Through practice and constant analysis of the game both on and off the ice, he has either been in, or imagined himself in just about every situation, time and time again. His repeated exposure means that he is rarely surprised. His concentration is not disturbed and he does not get distracted by things that distract other hockey players. He is able to let things go, to "make his mind like water." Because he does not get distracted at critical moments, Gretsky has greater awareness and anticipation. His experience has taught him where to look almost automatically and has helped him quiet his mind.

O.J. Simpson was football's equivalent to hockey's Wayne Gretsky. Like a great number of running backs "the Juice" learned that too much analysis leads to paralysis. O.J. often felt that he performed better in the second half of a football game, because by that time, he had calmed down and stopped thinking so much. The fatigue and the involvement in the game acted to shut off some of the internal distractions which kept him from seeing and hitting holes in the line.

The list of keys to total concentration is given below, followed by detailed explanation.

1. You must be able to shut off your own internal distractors. You have to be able to get rid of the sports commentator inside your head.
2. You must learn to identify and maintain your own optimal level of muscle tension and arousal. You must be able to differentiate muscle groups, tensing only those you need to tense at the proper time.
3. You must learn to attend passively to negative thoughts and feelings, either letting them go without worrying about them, or learning to use them to refocus attention on more positive, task-relevant cues.

OPTIMAL PERFORMANCE REQUIRES CONTROL OVER AROUSAL

Optimal performance and total concentration can only occur when your level of physical arousal matches the demands of the competitive situation. For each of us, there is a very fine line between being too aroused and not being aroused enough. Because controlling arousal is such an important part of your mental training, you need to fully understand what is meant by this concept.

The release of adrenalin from the adrenal glands causes a variety of physiological changes to occur. Included are increases in heart rate, respiration rate, blood pressure, and muscle tension. The changes in respiration and muscle tension can have profound effects on physical performance.

Too often, the assumption has been made that performance is best when the athlete is maximally aroused and the adrenalin is "really pumping." Maximal arousal is equated with maximal motivation. Many coaches make the mistake of considering arousal and motivation as being synonymous, and are always trying to "psych up" the athletes with whom they work. Some have become legendary for their eloquent pregame and halftime speeches which are supposed to heighten motivation.

Although this psyching up seems to work for certain individuals in certain situations, there are others for whom it has just the opposite effect. These athletes seem to have their best performance when they are relatively laid back or relaxed. Some athletes know that they need to *psych down* rather than *psych up*. What all this suggests is that each athlete has an optimal zone of arousal, and considerable research supports this observation.

OPTIMAL AROUSAL IS NOT EITHER/OR

Life would be simpler for coaches and athletes alike if we could label arousal as either good or bad. Unfortunately, we cannot do that. Although it makes things more complicated and requires a more careful analysis and preparation, accepting the fact that there are individual and situational differences that should determine your own optimal level of arousal will ultimately lead to performance improvement.

If your level of arousal becomes too low, you may lose interest, get bored, and not try as hard as you should. On the other hand, if your arousal is too high, you tighten up. Muscle tension increases to the point where you start working against yourself. You fatigue quicker, are more susceptible to cramps, and your movements become choppy. This interferes with your performance.

HIGH VERSUS LOW AROUSAL

1. The greater your level of self-confidence, the higher the level of arousal that you can tolerate, and the more likely you are to make mistakes because you were not aroused enough.

2. The more complicated the task, the less tolerance there will be for high levels of arousal. In sports like diving, gymnastics, and skating, which require analytical thinking, fine muscle coordination, and timing, problems occur most frequently because arousal levels are too high.

3. The shorter the duration of the performance, the more likely a high level of arousal will be beneficial because of the demand on gross muscle activity.

Although you can use these three general rules to get an idea of the level of arousal required by your sport (e.g., a higher level for a middle linebacker in football than for a golfer), you still need to refine your own assessment. You will need to be able to either shift rapidly from high levels of tension to low levels of tension (e.g., tensing muscles on entry for a dive but relaxing muscles on take off), or even more importantly, to differentiate levels of tension in specific muscle groups (e.g., tensing muscles that help you run or throw, while relaxing those that would be antagonistic).

The second part of your analysis should help you identify those specific muscle groups that are likely to be important to your performance. What parts of your body need to be tense and what parts need to be relaxed? Some specific questions you can use to identify what you need to do are provided below. (More will be said about this point in the next chapter.)

To examine the specific effects of increases and decreases in levels of muscle tension that are often involuntarily associated with changes in arousal, you should have a good idea of the importance of changes in breathing and in tension in muscles specific to your particular sport. For example, changes in breathing and changes in heart rate can have a critical influence on the performance of a shooter. These same changes may be relatively unimportant to a football player. With your own sport in mind, consider the following questions:

1. What muscle groups are critical to your performance? (e.g., in diving, in tennis, and in golf, tension in the chest, neck, and shoulders is critical.)

  _____
  _____
  _____
  _____
  _____

2. Which muscles should be tensed during performance and which ones should be relaxed?

  _____

_____

_____

_____

_____

3. Under pressure (e.g., at match point in a tennis match) are you able to maintain relaxation in those muscles that should be relaxed (e.g., shoulder muscles on the serve)?

_____

_____

_____

_____

_____

4. How important is rhythmic breathing? How closely associated is your breathing to correctly timing what you do? (e.g., to be breathing at the wrong time when jumping, shooting, etc., will interfere with your performance. In a team event like rowing, breathing at the wrong time can get you out of rhythm with the rest of the crew.)

_____

_____

_____

_____

5. Are you aware of what happens to your normal breathing pattern when you are under pressure? Does it cause you to inhale or exhale at times that affect performance?

_____

_____

_____

_____

_____

As you think about these questions, you should begin to see just how complicated the notion of optimal arousal really is. The fact that there are no simple answers is demonstrated by the photograph of Udo Byer taken just moments before he set a world record in the shot put (Figure 4.2).

Obviously, it takes a large dose of adrenalin and power to put the shot 73 feet. Nevertheless, Udo Byer has learned to control that flow of adrenalin so that it doesn't cause him to

FIGURE 4.2 Udo Byer moments before setting a world record in the shot put.

become too tense. Notice the relaxation in his left arm and hand just seconds before his world record put. By controlling antagonistic muscle tension and his breathing, Byer is able to take full advantage of the added explosiveness an increase in adrenalin can give. (If changes had occurred, they would have prevented him from maintaining the timing and the freedom of movement to get maximal effort.) His timing and coordination are not interfered with because the arousal has been directed to appropriate muscle groups rather than to simply increasing tension in general. As a result of this control, Byer sets a world record.

SHUTTING OUT NEGATIVE THOUGHTS— MAKING THEM POSITIVES

Competitors like Byer and Tom Petranoff are not only capable of differentiating muscle tension and breathing from other changes that may be associated with an increased adrenalin flow, they are also able to positively interpret those other changes. As an example, for most of us a pounding heart, sweaty palms, or a nervous stomach are cause for concern. When we experience these physical changes our thoughts become negative because we begin to have some doubts about our ability to function well. "Oh, oh, I'm getting nervous. Hope I can control myself and hold it together. Hope I don't get sick." These thoughts, when they occur, act to increase our anxiety even more and to dramatically interfere with our ability to control and to differentiate muscle tension levels and breathing. We become so preoccupied with our concerns and worries that we forget to check our feelings.

For Tom Petranoff, however, a pounding heart is a positive sign. When he is standing at the head of the runway, he waits to feel his heart because that is the cue that tells him he is concentrating and is able to focus on one thing. He knows that his adrenalin is flowing. Coincidentally, that is also the cue that reminds him to check his muscle tension, to make sure that he is relaxing the muscles in his shoulder and arm. In effect, Petranoff has taken what would be a negative signal to most of us and used it to his advantage.

SUMMARY

Chapter 4 discusses the following three keys to learning total concentration and to performing at your optimal level:

1. Learn to shut off the internal distractors.
2. Learn to identify and to maintain your own optimal level of muscle tension and arousal.
3. Learn to attend passively to negative thoughts and feelings and ultimately to turn them into cues to remind you to make needed adjustments in your arousal.

5

A Time for Analyzing

Although the last chapter stressed the importance of learning to shut off the commentator in your head, there are times when it is critical to talk to yourself. You must learn when and when not to talk to yourself. Effective performers use self-talk and self-analysis for the following reasons.

1. They maintain a high level of motivation and task involvement. A good talking to, *at the right time*, can be very effective in getting you "back into the game."
2. They focus concentration on the task at hand.
3. They learn new skills. Before performance has become automatic, or when we need to change automatic performance in order to improve our technique, the use of self-instructions is critical. It is through conscious reminders and self-instructions that we practice the type of concentration required by new situations. Once you overlearn both the physical and mental response so that your performance becomes automatic, you will want to shut off these self-instructions.
4. They analyze and plan for the future to learn from past mistakes. An athlete who wants to avoid making the same mistakes repeatedly must take the time to assess and to analyze the conditions that are leading to the problem.

A persistent stereotype in sport is the belief that top athletes do not make good coaches and vice-versa. Whether this statement is true or not, the attentional demands placed on a coach are often quite different from the demands placed on an athlete. Top-level competitors are expected to have developed their physical skills to the point where execution can be automatic. When this is the case, the demand on the athlete is to attend to the environment, to the competitive situation so that he or she will be ready to react automatically to the performance requirements. The athlete has to be involved in the here and now.

In contrast, coaches must be able to respond to a different set of task demands. First, they must function as teachers. They must be doing the analysis for which the athlete does not have time. Coaches are responsible for teaching athletes what to pay attention to and what to avoid. To be good teachers, coaches must be analytical. They must spend considerable time mentally analyzing information, problem solving, and developing communication strategies with athletes and others.

While the players are busy reacting to a developing play, coaches should be analyzing what is happening. As a play develops, a good coach is absorbing information for immediate or subsequent analysis. He must be able to make substitutions, to adjust to unexpected circumstances and to plan for future developments.

Ideally, coach and athlete alike are equally adept at concentrating on the environment (reacting) and at analyzing (problem solving). This special combination exists in athletes whose sports give them time for analysis. For example, Dwight Stones probably knows more about his event (high jump) and his own performance than any coach ever will. The fact that he has some control over when he will approach the bar gives him the time he needs to be more analytical. In a sport like boxing or sprints, analysis at the time you are performing is more difficult.

Differences between individuals present difficulties as well. Some athletes are much more analytical than others, independent of the sport situation. These individuals are good at analyzing and have been successful in the past in using their ability to analyze, to problem solve, and to improve. Although these athletes may also be capable of reacting quickly to the competitive situation, as pressure increases so does the likelihood that they will become too analytical.

In contrast, other athletes do very little analyzing. They have had their success because they reacted quickly and automatically to the events in the contest. When they are not under pressure, they are quite capable of analyzing situations. As pressure increases, however, they play to their strength. They have a tendency to react impulsively and to repeat the same mistake. Like the running back who has a problem fumbling the football, they put themselves on automatic and the little voice that should remind them to hold onto the ball is never heard from.

If there is any truth to the belief that good coaches do not make good athletes and vice-versa, it is because these individuals have been content to allow themselves to be dominated by their own particular attentional strengths. They have failed to perceive the need to become more or less analytical under pressure. They have not bothered, or have not been given the opportunity, to learn how to gain greater attentional control, how to shift back and forth from an analytical to a reactive focus of attention. The trick is to learn *when* to be analytical.

This chapter will help you to determine when you should be analytical and when you need to stop the analytical process; in addition, it will help you become more effective in your analysis by teaching you what to attend to.

WHEN SHOULD YOU BE ANALYTICAL?

I have found some general rules which can guide you for when it is appropriate to be analytical and when it is not. Being analytical is useful when you are first learning a new skill. The development of proper motor control, learning various motor sequences, and learning when to take a shot in basketball or to pass to a teammate, requires conscious thought and rehearsal at the beginning.

The pressure to perform perfectly the first time or to learn the skill very quickly is the biggest problem most athletes have. They place emphasis on performing, not on learning.

This pressure keeps athletes from taking the time to analyze the skill and to remind themselves of the various things they need to do. As a result, athletes tend to make the same mistakes over and over. By eliminating the pressure to perform perfectly, athletes give themselves the time needed to analyze.

The ideal time to analyze is outside of the competitive situation when the game is over or when the point has been played. This is particularly true if your performance is "automatic." It is after the fact, when thoughts do not become distractions for current or subsequent performance that you can review the game films (literally or figuratively). This applies especially if you lack confidence and your arousal level is high. The more doubts you have and the more aroused you are, the greater difficulty you will have shifting from the internal, analytical type of attention back to the external, reactive one.

The next best time to analyze is during practice. The reason for this is that the goals in practice typically are more supportive of analytical thinking. You are rewarded or congratulated for thinking and for making changes or for learning new things. The focus in practice is not as likely to be on the outcome of a game because primary importance is given instead to skill development. Practice also provides the opportunity for taking time out. Often, you can stop in the middle of something you are doing and start over. This gives you time to analyze. In this way, the pressure to react or to complete the analysis in a short period of time is removed.

Exercise caution in being analytical during the game. First, you must identify times during the contest when you will have the opportunity to be analytical without feeling rushed. Obviously, that is not when you are in the middle of shooting, hitting, throwing, catching, for example. Second, if you expect to use the analysis to make changes, be prepared for some reduction in your ability to perform. For example, if I asked you to think about how tense your muscles were just as you got ready to serve in tennis, those thoughts would serve as a distraction, interfering with your normal rhythm and timing. You might very well learn something about muscle tension, but at that moment, it would be at the expense of performance.

Too often, athletes who attempt to be analytical during a performance situation end up behaving in impulsive, superstitious ways that completely disrupt what they are trying to do, as in this example from tennis: In a warm-up just before a match, a player noticed that her volleys were going long. The prematch warm-up only gave her a few minutes to hit each of a variety of shots (serves, volleys, ground strokes, overheads). When the volleys started going long, she attempted to analyze her technique. Unfortunately, other thoughts disrupted her analysis. Just as she would start to problem solve, a thought would come in telling her that she did not have much time left. These distractions forced her to start the analysis again, causing her to physically tighten up. Because of the delay, time was even more of a factor at this point. In desperation, the athlete impulsively started changing her stroke. These changes did not help, and, as a result, she entered the match without any confidence in her volley. Had she not tried to be so analytical under pressured circumstances, all of this could have been avoided.

We often hear coaches say that preseason won-lost records are not that important. When you view preseason games as times to be analytical because the pressure of winning is off in order to have the opportunity to learn, it can be to your advantage. Under these circumstances, losses during preseason lead to wins during the regular season.

The implication here is that you should not allow yourself to analyze in a game unless you are willing to place the goals of learning and of future development ahead of immediate performance. Obviously, some of the learning that you would like to do must occur in the contest. By going into the contest with the attitude that learning is more important, and that now is the time to make mistakes from which to learn, you will increase your chances for later success.

Later I will ask you to learn something about yourself during competition. This self-discovery may suggest the need for you to change what you think about or attend to as you perform. To take the pressure off yourself, and to increase the likelihood that you will be able to follow my suggestions, you will need to select a competitive situation that is relatively unimportant. You may also need to get the support of your coach or teammates to help you make this change. Sometimes, however, problems can develop.

In talking with a swimmer we determined that a particular meet was relatively unimportant. Because his performance would not affect the conference standings, the ultimate team score, or his qualifying for nationals, it provided the opportunity to try to change his normal racing strategy. The problem was that he felt he could swim faster than he had been doing, but fear of burning out during the middle of the race kept him from pushing himself sooner. We decided to use this particular race to test his limits. "It doesn't matter if you lose or burn out. All that matters is that we find out (a) if you can push yourself to swim faster during the middle of a race, and (b) if you can, will you burn out?" We jointly established his goal which consisted of swimming the first 50 meters in the same time he normally did, then to drop his time in the second and third 50s by 3 seconds, and to see if he would be able to carry his speed through the final 50.

Although we had planned everything, when the day of the meet arrived, things got sabotaged. The athlete's parents and girl friend showed up and expected him to win. The team set a team goal of getting a certain number of points. For the team to accomplish its goal, he would have to win his race. As a result, the outside pressure kept him from following through with our plan. He swam his usual conservative race, not wanting to lose in front of his parents and girl friend. Sometimes you will have to forego immediate success to accomplish changes.

WHAT SHOULD YOU BE ANALYZING?

The amount of information that any of us can deal with at one time is limited. You probably can remember and repeat a single seven-digit phone number when it is presented to you for the first time, but I doubt if you would accurately remember and repeat two seven-digit phone numbers when they are presented as a string of 14 numbers.

To compensate for limited processing ability, great coaches and athletes have come to know what to attend to, and what to avoid. Either through a tremendous amount of practice and training, or at some "unconscious" level, they have developed explicit or implicit strategies for identifying and attending to critical or task-relevant cues.

However, even great athletes, entering a new competitive situation for the first time, have a tendency to become distracted by cues that are irrelevant to performance. Some of these may be external (e.g., noticing the crowd), others internal (e.g., noticing their own anxiety). Because it is a new situation, the athlete has not yet learned what to attend to. Thinking back on some of your own experiences, you may be able to recall that in new situations you had a tendency to attend to simply too many things. The pressure we feel and our lack of knowledge causes us to treat irrelevant cues as if they were relevant. In effect, we get "faked out." In football, the athlete reacts to a head fake by a runner because he has not yet learned to avoid reacting to that cue. He has not learned that the relevant thing to attend to is the runner's center of gravity.

Often, analytical athletes are quick learners—that is because associated with good analytical ability is the facility to systematically organize and evaluate information. Those people who we identify as the intellectuals of sport are individuals who have a plan for analyzing the things they see. Often, we do not know what their plan is; but we do know they have a more effective way of looking at things than we do. Somehow, they have identified the critical cues that help them predict what will happen under different sets of conditions.

Although the great coach may not be able to tell his athletes exactly what it is they are observing that allows them to say the right thing at the right time, it is not that big of a mystery. These individuals are able to sense when (a) an athlete's arousal level is too high or too low, or (b) the individual is spending too much time in the head versus not thinking enough.

Chapter 4 pointed out how muscle tension in various muscle groups (e.g., neck, shoulders, etc.) often provides a good indication that arousal levels are too high, and how you could become sensitive to those levels of tension. Now let me give you something else to attend to that will help you recognize when performance problems are likely to occur: Use your own analytical ability to help you improve performance by identifying what you need to think about when you are having problems controlling arousal and/or concentration. Great coaches can see if your level of tension is too high or too low. They realize when you are too analytical or too reactive, and know what to say or do to counteract your problem.

The remaining chapters will help you see exactly what it is that you need to do to gain control (e.g., to alter muscle tension and to concentrate). Here are a few general rules that many great coaches follow:

1. If athletes' arousal levels are too high, and if they are worried about the competition (e.g., they have a low level of self-confidence), get them to concentrate on the act of competing, forgetting about the outcome.

2. If arousal is too low, challenge the athletes. To motivate them, remind them of consequences of failure and of their lack of commitment. Focus on outcome and on their obligation to themselves and others.

3. If athletes are angry and are reacting in frustration and irritation to things going on around them (e.g., blaming others for problems, yelling at officials, committing dumb fouls), confront them. Encourage them to become more analytical, to go inside of their heads, and to think about their behavior. Get them to take time out to regain control so that they can become more logical and analytical.

If athletes are worried, seem depressed, or have gone inside their heads and are slow to react to the game, you need to draw them out. Often, this is accomplished better through reassurance and support than it is through confrontation. Help them to stop the analysis that is going on and instead provide some external structure like one or two critical performance cues to which they should attend.

SUMMARY

In chapter 5 you learned *when* you should be "inside your head," analyzing your own performance. Analytical thinking should occur (a) when you are trying to learn a new skill; and

(b) when you need to analyze your own performance in order to identify relative strengths and weaknesses to refine training programs. You are better off if you engage in analytical thinking during practice situations when you can take the time required and when the pressure to win is removed.

In addition *what* you pay attention to when trying to determine how to improve performance is critical:

1. You need to attend to muscle tension levels in those muscle groups that are directly related to performance.
2. You need to be sensitive to your own tendency to become too analytical versus not analytical enough.

In the next chapter, you will find out about mental rehearsal techniques. These are procedures that you can use to improve your ability to be analytical.

6

Mental Rehearsal

In recent years, a wide variety of mental imagery techniques have been applied to sport. Words like *mental rehearsal, positive thinking, success visualization, visual motor behavior rehearsal, cognitive behavior modification, and imagery* have all been used to describe procedures for altering thoughts, feelings, attitudes, and performance.

The use of imagery, however, is not new! Athletes have engaged in mental practice for as long as they have been involved in sport. In fact, research shows that better athletes have better recall for what goes on in their sport. Top skiers, for example, can make one run down a course and remember many more details about the course than intermediate skiers. In addition, better athletes, when they mentally rehearse certain sport skills which are associated with the passage of time, seem to rehearse much more closely to "real time." By real time, I mean that the length of time it takes to rehearse the activity is the same as the time it actually takes to carry out the activity.

The ability to rehearse in real time is a critical part of top-level performance. Pressure and anxiety have a tendency to disrupt our internal clocks and, as a result, coordination and timing suffer. Athletes go out too fast and have difficulty pacing themselves. When individuals are capable of rehearsing in real time, anxiety is much less likely to disrupt performance, and they seem to have a greater tolerance for pressure.

The biggest problem with mental rehearsal techniques lies in clearly knowing what you want to rehearse. There are many different types of imagery and rehearsal, and each of them can be of assistance in learning and refining your performance.

In this chapter you will learn some of the different ways you can image and rehearse your performance. Later you will be examining each procedure in detail with specific goals in mind (e.g., to learn to be able to recover quickly from the unexpected in the middle of a competition).

WHAT ARE YOUR IMAGERY SKILLS?

Read this paragraph and then complete the mental exercise before you move on. Begin by closing your eyes and by imagining that you are getting up. You stand up and move across the room. Once you reach the other side, turn around and walk back to the chair or couch on which you were sitting and take your seat. Complete this mental exercise now, before going any further!

Having completed the exercise, answer the questions in the following checklist:

Mental Rehearsal Checklist

	Yes	No
1. Were you able to get clear, vivid images?	☐	☐
2. Were the images in color?	☐	☐
3. Did you see a series of snapshots?	☐	☐
4. Did action proceed like a movie (e.g., continuous action as opposed to snapshots)?	☐	☐
5. In your mind were you an observer, watching yourself perform (like you would watch an actor or actress in a movie)?	☐	☐

6. In your mind were you the actor? Were you mentally rehearsing from the perspective you would have if you were inside your own body? From this perspective you would not be able to see your own face. □   □

7. When you imagined yourself moving, were you able to actually feel the movements? Did you feel the tension levels change in the muscles that would be working? □   □

Humans have vastly different imagery abilities, especially when it comes to visual imagery. Some people have great difficulty developing and holding a visual image. They get brief flashes of the outline of the image and then, if they want to analyze it, they have to do that by remembering feelings and thoughts associated with different parts of the image. For others, the images are as vivid and real as those on any movie screen.

The particular perspective you take when you attempt to rehearse or analyze a situation can be very important. For example, the use of imagery to develop physical skills and to speed motor learning will be more successful if you actively rehearse the physical feelings or kinesthetic feelings associated with the movements. To do this, you take the perspective you would have if you were actually performing the activity.

Now take the imagery test you just took, only this time I am going to direct your rehearsal process a little more. In fact, you can begin rehearsing while reading the next few paragraphs. This means you can mentally rehearse without closing your eyes. Some people find it easier with their eyes open.

I want you to see yourself closing the book and placing it off to the side. As you imagine yourself closing the book, do it from inside your own body. Just look at the book and imagine closing it. As you imagine closing it, I want you to concentrate on feeling the muscles in your hands, and forearms contracting in the way they would contract if you actually create small muscle movements that mimic those associated with closing the book.

Now, as you mentally place the book off to the side, again concentrate on feeling the muscle movements. Next, I want you to imagine that you are standing up. Again, with eyes open, look in the direction you would look if you were standing up. What part of your body would move first, your head as you lean forward, your arms, neck, shoulders? I want you to feel each part of your body as it moves. As you stand up, see if you can feel the knees straighten. Can you feel the increased tension in calf and thigh muscles?

Next, begin to walk across the room (without actually leaving your chair). Feel the movement in your legs and your arms. As you reach the other side, pay attention to the muscles in your body as you turn. Can you feel the movement of your hips and shoulders? Can you feel yourself turn on the balls of your feet?

Return to the chair and feel all of the movements as you turn, sit down and move yourself back into a comfortable position. Pick the book back up, open it, and continue with your reading.

How did you do with this exercise? Were you able to create the feelings? Take the time to once again answer the questions in the checklist.

Mental Rehearsal Checklist

	Yes	No
1. Were you able to get clear, vivid images?	☐	☐
2. Were the images in color?	☐	☐
3. Did you see a series of snapshots?	☐	☐
4. Did action proceed like a movie (e.g., continuous action as opposed to snapshots)?	☐	☐
5. In your mind were you an observer, watching yourself perform (like you would watch an actor or actress in a movie)?	☐	☐

6. In your mind were you the actor? Were you mentally rehearsing from the perspective you would have if you were inside your own body? From this perspective you would not be able to see your own face.   ☐   ☐

7. When you imagined yourself moving, were you able to actually feel the movements? Did you feel the tension levels change in the muscles that would be working?   ☐   ☐

Let us try one more exercise. This one requires a stopwatch, or at least a watch with a second hand. What I want you to do is to test your ability to rehearse in real time under two conditions.

First, attempt to see yourself getting up out of a chair, walking across the room, turning around and returning to the chair, but imagine it with your *eyes closed*. Start timing when you close your eyes and stop timing when you imagine yourself sitting back down and picking up the book. Complete that part of the exercise now.

Next, time yourself again, only this time do it with your *eyes open*. Go through the same imagery process but allow yourself to take advantage of the actual visual cues in the room. Once again, start the timing as you mentally begin to close the book and stop timing when you have returned to the chair and reopened the book.

Finally, actually engage in the activity of shutting the book, standing up, moving across the room, returning to the chair and reopening the book. Time how long the actual activity takes you. How accurate were your imagined attempts?

The greater the discrepancy between your imagined time and real time, the more likely you need to work on developing a greater feel for what you are doing. This is especially true if you are rehearsing some aspect of sport performance. In fact, why not compare your ability to rehearse some physical aspect of performance to the exercise you just completed? For example, a basketball player might rehearse stepping to the free-throw line and taking a shot; a diver might rehearse a particular dive; a golfer could rehearse teeing up the ball and completing a drive; a wide receiver in football might rehearse running a particular pass pattern. Select your activity and rehearse it.

Next, get someone to time the actual activity as you perform. Are you more or less as capable of rehearsing a highly polished skill in real time than you were of rehearsing the walk across the room? Remember, the greater the discrepancy between the actual time it takes and the time it takes you to mentally rehearse in real time, the more likely your timing will be interfered with under pressure.

As an example of this process, I asked a team of four parachutists to mentally rehearse a sequence of five formations they would have to make while free-falling at over 120 miles an hour. I asked the team leader to call out the shifts in the formations as they occurred and then asked the team as a group if the rehearsal had been in real time. They all said no; the rehearsal had been 2 to 3 times faster than actual speed. As a result, I asked them to rehearse the sequence again, attempting to practice at real speed. Once again, the team captain called out the shifts. As they rehearsed the jump, I timed it. When rehearsal was complete, I asked them how long the time period would actually be; I also asked them if they had been rehearsing at that rate. They all agreed that rehearsal had been occurring at real time. When I compared their estimate of the time to the actual elapsed time, they were within .5 seconds. In this instance, four highly skilled athletes were right together!

The next chapters will teach you to use different forms of mental imagery for a variety of tasks. Different forms mean different aspects of the rehearsal process (e.g., the kinesthetic or motor feelings, the images generated when you are the actor, etc.). The tasks will be as follows:

1. To learn to control attention so that you can sleep prior to a competition, and so that you can prevent burning up valuable emotional and physical energy reserves needed for the competition.

2. To learn to improve imagery and memory through the use of relaxation procedures and the use of structured questions.

3. To use imagery to identify your own optimal level of arousal.

4. To learn to center and to control breathing as a basis for "making your mind like water" and "focusing your ki" and to test your ability to center and to focus ki.

5. To learn to use rehearsal processes to speed the learning of physical (motor) skills, and to rapidly automate performance.

6. To learn to use rehearsal processes to stop negative thinking and to focus on positive imagery and more task-relevant cues.

7. To use centering and rehearsal to prevent becoming distracted by irrelevant thoughts and external distractors. Using mental simulation of performance to anticipate and prevent problems.

SUMMARY

Chapter 7 discusses ways of using imagery and performance rehearsal. A checklist gives the reader the opportunity to assess his or her individual capability for imagery. Each athlete needs to identify *what* should be rehearsed and *when* and *how* the training should take place. What is right for one person may not be useful for another.

It is also important that the *perspective* taken during imagery and mental rehearsal be tailored to the specific sport situation:

1. To develop physical skill and speed motor-learning, rehearse the physical or kinesthetic feelings associated with the movements, and take the perspective of yourself performing the activity.

2. To develop better timing and to learn to adjust the imagined time to the "real time," use the perspective of an onlooker observing you in action.

Chapter 7 will teach the use of different forms of mental imagery for specific tasks.

7

Improving Your Ability to Image

Although a great deal of research and practical experience support the systematic use of imagery and mental rehearsal, few athletes have taken full advantage of this fact. Interviews with top divers, ice hockey and field hockey players, swimmers, and gymnasts indicate that almost 98% use some type of imagery. There are tremendous differences between these athletes, however, with respect to their imagery skills.

A diver like Greg Louganis (Figure 7.1) has very highly developed rehearsal skills. Louganis continually rehearses his dives. He is thinking about them away from the pool, between dives during competition, and when he is actually on the board or platform. He goes over them very systematically again and again, rehearsing from several different perspectives. He can visualize himself doing the dive, or take the perspective of someone in the audience watching the dive. He can image from inside his own body, generating the kinesthetic feelings as well as the visual images. Finally, he rehearses to music, using the tempo and rhythm of the music to assist him in his timing and execution.

In contrast to Louganis, some other divers have not learned to rehearse at all. Often, these individuals have been exposed to the idea of thinking their way through their dives but have difficulty developing the images. They assume that other people see clear images and pictures, and when they do not, they decide that something must be wrong. "I just didn't think I was capable of imaging like the other divers."

FIGURE 7.1 Greg Louganis uses imagery extensively in practicing his dives. (International Swimming Hall of Fame, reproduced by permission)

The exercises in the previous chapter showed the differences in individual athletes' abilities to develop imagery and kinesthetic recall (the ability to know the position of your body in space). You may not be one of the fortunate few who seem to instinctively use rehearsal, but you can develop your mental abilities. *The athlete who can use visual, auditory, and kinesthetic cues to speed learning and facilitate timing and coordination is at a decided advantage*, especially as pressure increases. It is your own internal clock that will keep you from racing too fast, pressing too hard when anxiety makes the world around you seem speeded up.

ANXIETY DISRUPTS IMAGERY

One of the reasons that many athletes fail to develop good imagery skills is that rehearsal does not occur to them until they are almost ready to perform. These athletes wait until the competition has begun and then they attempt to think their way through their performance. It is very hard to control concentration when physiological arousal is high, especially if you have not practiced imagery! A discussion with another world class diver illustrates this point.

I had asked this diver the following question to determine if he could tell the difference between his feelings in practice and his feelings in competition: "In practice just before doing a dive, can you tell when you are feeling confident and in control?" He said he could and described the different feelings in muscle groups as follows:

> Standing on the board I feel steady and solid, like a triangle sitting on its base. The board seems very wide and the thought of falling off to the side doesn't even enter my mind. When I am not confident, however, I feel like a triangle standing on its head. I feel shaky, the board seems narrower. I don't feel the same control. As I make my approach toward the end of the board, I feel as if I could be pushed off balance quite easily. I am not sure when I go up on my hurdle step if I will come back down in the center of the board or not.

When I asked the same diver if he could detect similar differences during competition, he could not! In competition, he became so "reved up" that the noise in his own body (e.g., increasing muscle tension, rapid heart rate) and his own distracting thoughts kept him from being as sensitive as he should be to his own optimal level of arousal. As a result, his performance was more erratic in competition.

One of the first things that you should do to begin to develop your imagery is to practice under relatively nonstressful conditions. This is one of the reasons that some sport psychologists combine imagery and relaxation procedures. By helping athletes reduce external distractions (noise, sights), and by lowering their physiological arousal (reducing internal distractions like muscle tension and negative thoughts), they are able to use their imagery skills better. You can develop your imagery skills by first rehearsing away from the competition where you are not distracted. Once you are able to image well under these relaxed conditions, you can proceed to use imagery in practices and then at selected times during actual competition.

YOU NEED STRUCTURE

When first using imagery, many athletes cannot decide on what to focus and therefore lack structure. As arousal and anxiety increase, athletes jump rapidly from one thing to another. The world becomes little more than a blur. The hitter in baseball gets into the batter's box and suddenly an 80 mile per hour pitch seems like it is coming at 100. The diver doing a back 3½ off the 10-meter tower attempts to "spot the dive" by seeing the back of the tower each time she spins in order to time her opening. All too often, her anxiety prevents her from spotting anything: All she can see is a blur.

Ted Williams reported he could see the baseball make contact with the bat, yet scientists maintain that such a perceptual feat is impossible. As a former diver and a scientist, I would have said that the ability to see anything clearly when spinning fast enough to execute a 3½ somersault would be impossible. However, I have learned that others have taught themselves to see things I could not. After talking with Ron O'Brien, the coach of our 1984 Olympic divers, I know that the divers can spot those dives. Some divers cannot only see the tower, but can actually read a sign with a five-digit number on it. When I was diving, I was a victim of my own anxiety and disbelief, unable to take advantage of information that was available to me.

Seeing, processing, and reacting to information can occur in an incredibly short period of time. The key to making the right decisions and to reacting appropriately involves knowing what to look for, and when to look for it. If you were to watch slow motion pictures of Greg Louganis during a complicated dive, you could see his head move up and down as he briefly holds position in order to spot his dives. We can speculate that Greg's internal clock, his highly developed sense of rhythm, aided by his mental rehearsal and his pairing up of music with that rehearsal, helps him time his looks on the actual dive. By moving his head at just the right time, he is able to hold attention on the tower longer than other divers. He gets a clear image, and he is able to use that image to tell him when to open on the dive.

Greg Louganis has a systematic way of mentally rehearsing, which includes taking different perspectives from inside and outside his own body, using kinesthetic and visual cues that he will feel and see while diving, and using auditory recall aided by music to help his timing. His rehearsal is highly structured, being much more sophisticated than most athletes'. Your imagery need not be so finely tuned, especially when you are just beginning. The following list will help you find some general ways of increasing the structure and focus of your own rehearsal process. In this way, you can enhance the imagery and the usefulness of your practice.

1. Make a decision as to the desired perspective. Obviously, what you attempt to see and to feel will depend on whether you are "in the audience" or actually performing. At first, practice the two perspectives independently; later you can begin to combine them.

2. Decide in advance what it is you need to pay attention to. Which movements, feelings, or times in the performance need to be emphasized? Establish a rehearsal goal. For example, is it your goal to become more sensitive to levels of muscle tension? If it is, you will direct attention towards relevant muscle groups and ignore many

other cues. Is it your goal to be able to "spot a dive"? In this case, you will need to concentrate on visual cues rather than kinesthetic ones.

MAKE USE OF MEMORY AIDS

How many times have you walked down the street and suddenly smelled something that caused a flood of old memories? Perhaps a particular odor reminded you of a meal at someone's house 10 years before. Maybe you have had the experience of having a sound suddenly cause you to remember something from the past. Somehow the smell or sound triggers a whole scene for you. Memories and images are linked together in our senses and, as a result, cues from one sense can help stimulate others. We can use feelings to help us create visual images, and we can use visual images to help us create feelings.

I had a rower tell me she had been unable to use any visual imagery as a practice device until she accidentally paired her thoughts with actual feelings. She was sitting on the floor with her legs straight out in front of her. She leaned forward as if to take a stroke and found herself both feeling and imaging rowing. She had inadvertently used physical cues and recall to stimulate mental images.

Below is a brief list of some of the memory aids you can use to help facilitate recall of experiences:

1. Use actual physical cues. Begin by going through the particular movements that are critical. You may not be able to recreate the entire sequence. If you cannot, begin with the most obvious cues. These would include at the beginning of the entire performance sequence, at any *transition points*, places where you change the direction of movement, and at the end of the performance sequence. As an example, a baseball pitcher would begin by recalling and actually initiating the rocking movement as he starts his wind-up. He would attend to the transition in the wind-up between leaning backwards and then shifting his body forward as he begins the delivery. Finally, he would zero in on the follow-through.

2. Once you have created the movements by actually going through them, sit down and close your eyes. Try and use a series of much smaller movements to recreate for yourself both the feelings and the images. For example, a slight almost imperceptible nod of the head might provide the pitcher with enough of a kinesthetic cue to allow for the recall of the rest of the motor sequence. In addition to a slight movement at the beginning, try and sense slight movements as you mentally rehearse the transitions (changes in movement direction).

3. You can use external visual cues to help you develop both visual imagery and kinesthetic recall. Take your actual position in the competitive situation. You need not have anyone else involved; in fact, it may be better to be alone. Standing in position without any pressure on you, take the time to recreate the competitive conditions. Actually look out at the field and attempt to see what you would see. You can facilitate your ability to image by pairing what you are looking at with slight movements. This is what Dwight Stones, the high jumper, does when he images his approach to the high-jump bar. If you watch, you will see him standing with his eyes open. He will look at the bar and then he will look towards the position on the ground where he will place his foot as he makes his first step. Watching him, you can see by his nodding head and slight movements in arms and legs that he is actually creating for himself both the kinesthetic and visual cues that he will feel and see once he makes his actual approach. Dwight is using the structure provided by the competitive situation. This includes the position of the high-jump pit and bar, as well as his own body position to aid his mental rehearsal.

4. You can use external visual cues from the audience's perspective to assist in developing imagery and recall. Watch someone else, or a video-tape of yourself, engaging in the activity that you want to rehearse. As you watch, key in on the start, the transition points, and the end. Time your movements to coincide with the model and see if you can feel what he or she feels. For example,

watching Dwight Stones, you would begin to nod your head with him. As he approaches the bar and transfers his horizontal speed into his take off, you would attempt to feel your own leg drive you up and over the bar. Once you create these feelings with observations, reduce the number of memory aids and visual cues, and try and create the images and feelings inside your head. Close your eyes and rehearse on your own.

5. Experiment to see how capable you are of using auditory cues, like music, to help you develop certain images and feelings. You can approach this in a couple of ways: First, you can listen to various pieces of music and try to imagine the feelings and/or images that you might associate with the music; second, and perhaps easier, you can watch the performance, especially an "inspirational performance," and then fit music to it. The key is to pair the music to your own performance. I have run 10 kilometer races where the theme from *Rocky* has been played as the runners approached the top of a hill. The goal of the race organizers has been to pair the feelings of confidence and conquest associated with the music and the image of Rocky with the runner's own efforts. When it works, it is a very powerful tool for turning negative attention such as doubts into very positive directions. On these occasions, the images and auditory cues have become personal motivators.

However, a word of caution here about listening to music. Some evidence shows that arousal levels fluctuate almost involuntarily with music. For example, fights at hockey matches last longer when the music being played at the time is of the Rocky type. Likewise, emotions cool more quickly when the music is more soothing.

As an athlete, you can take advantage of this fact to help yourself control arousal. I have told athletes in the past to change the music they listen to following a competition when they must be ready to compete again within a few hours or within a day. Often, I will have athletes listen to their favorite rock music just prior to a competition if they are trying to get up. If they are too aroused, however, I will ask them to slow the music, their own movements, and their talking. All of these things help in calming them down.

IDENTIFYING YOUR OPTIMAL LEVEL OF AROUSAL

Use some of the suggestions that were just made to help you learn to recognize and control your own optimal level of arousal! As I mentioned, it is extremely difficult to control something of which you are not aware. Optimal performance requires each of us to walk that fine line between over and under arousal.

The first thing to do in order to become more sensitive to yourself is to begin analyzing under relatively nonstressful conditions. The last thing you need is one more thing to talk about when you are trying to perform. By thinking about past performance now, outside of the competitive situation, you should be able to reduce distractions and be able to concentrate and recall important information.

In addition to recalling important information, you need some structure so that you attend to the right cues. This means attending specifically to those physiological cues (feelings of tension or lack of it in particular muscle groups) and mental cues (confidence indicators) that are likely to be associated with alterations in arousal, and at the same time, related to performance.

1. Begin by identifying two performance situations, similar in performance demands but dissimilar in terms of outcome. In one, you performed very well; in the other, you performed poorly.

2. Next, identify those muscle groups that are critical to effective performance in the two situations. It is very important that you identify both the muscles that need to be contracted and used to initiate action, as well as those that need to be relaxed in order to avoid interfering. *This is a critical point.* Often, athletes are sensitive to the muscles that facilitate an activity but pay very little attention to those that inhibit it (until they become painfully obvious). Look to relatively large muscle groups first, for example, muscles in the neck and shoulders, thigh muscles, calf muscles, and so on. Ask yourself if there are particular muscle groups in your sport that are especially important (e.g., tension in

forearms in shooting or tension in the fingers and hand in the javelin). Which muscles, if tightened, will interfere with your performance? What effect will their tightening up have on the body? For example, excessive tension in the legs and upper body might cause a sprinter to straighten up and interfere with the lean at the tape. Excessive tension in the hands and fingers of a wide receiver could reduce the sensitivity and flexibility of his hands causing the ball to bounce off.

You must attempt to mentally recreate the two experiences and contrast them. To do this, use some of the ideas about structure that were presented earlier. The goal is to identify *discriminate cues* or those feelings that separate the two experiences. Obviously, there will be a large number of differences, so the real key involves identifying those that are most performance relevant.

Start with the physical cues. Close your eyes and recreate the successful experience in your own mind. Do this by attending to the feelings you had in critical muscle groups immediately prior to beginning the performance sequence. Next, see if you can sense the feelings in critical muscle groups at the transition points, and, finally, check the tension levels at the end of the sequence.

If you find that you are having difficulty recreating these feelings, stand up and go through the movements, and get into the actual situation so you can use some external structural cues as well as your own physical feelings to help stimulate the memories. Check the tension levels in muscles that are supposed to be relatively relaxed. Now, use the rating scale below to provide yourself with a benchmark against which to evaluate tension.

Think of your level of tension on a 10-point scale. Completely loose, as relaxed as a rag doll, would be represented by the number 1. A 5 would indicate the approximate level of arousal at which you spend most of your "just walking around" time. Think of 10 as being so tight that your body would feel absolutely rigid and brittle.

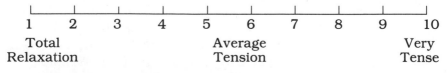

Assign a number to the tension level in the critical muscle groups during a successful performance situation; then, recreate the images and feelings associated with a poor performance. Check your tension level in the critical muscle groups and indicate a number.

If you find that you are unable to recall those past situations, you will have to begin by examining current tension levels in actual practice situations. Pick a time when the goal can be to identify optimal tension levels rather than to perform at your "best." Go into the situation with only that goal in mind; mentally check tension levels just before starting a response, at the transition points, and at the conclusion of the performance sequence. Remember, unless you are willing to engage in this process and train yourself to the type of sensitivity to which I am referring, you cannot make effective use of the techniques to follow.

SUMMARY

Chapter 7 demonstrates that it is possible to *develop* good imagery and rehearsal skills. These skills will act to improve the consistency of your performance. To develop your own skills, you need to keep the following points in mind:

1. Begin rehearsing under nonstressful conditions in a place without auditory and visual distractors. You may also want to use a relaxation procedure to help reduce distractions.

2. Develop a structure or strategy that will help you determine what it is that you should attend to and rehearse. Knowing where to look is critical; you want to rehearse attending to the right cues, not the wrong ones.

3. Determine your optimal level of arousal and attend to those physiological cues (indicators of muscle tension) that are directly related to performance.

4. Make use of memory aids. External cues and/or internal images will help you recall physical sensations; auditory cues can help to develop visual images or vice versa.

5. Check to see if you have discovered those "discriminate cues" that tell you when you are too tense; systematically contrast successful performance situations with unsuccessful ones. Use imagery to recall them and to contrast the feelings and sensations associated with them.

Chapter 8 will show how controlling what you attend to can be used to cope with anxiety before competition, for example, the very common problem of sleeplessness.

8

Relaxation Prior to Major Competition

Some athletes can appear so calm once the competition begins and yet were so anxious several nights before that they could not sleep! The problem of not being able to sleep occurs for several good reasons.

When athletes attempt to "peak" for a major competition, they typically have a period of lighter training immediately prior to the competition. This rest from strenuous training allows energy to build up and athletes simply are not as fatigued as they normally might be. Experienced athletes find themselves with an excess of energy and time on their hands.

Without the normal training demands to occupy their thoughts, they are free to ruminate and worry about the upcoming competition. They begin to analyze their own preparation, to second-guess what they have been doing. Their active minds seem unable to rest and they cannot get away from worries. They begin to fret because they are not sleeping, and then they worry about worrying. It all seems a vicious circle.

If experienced athletes could avoid the worry about not sleeping and would simply lie quietly for a few hours each day, they would be fine. They do not really need 8-10 hours of sleep every night. Unfortunately, when their normal sleeping pattern is disturbed, they begin worrying and this burns up valuable emotional and physical energy. Thus, even experienced athletes can find themselves exhausted and flat when the competition finally rolls around. The worry over not sleeping has created the problem, not the lack of sleep.

If you understand that each of us has an identifiable "sleep cycle," you may worry less about the restlessness you feel on nights before major competitions. Typically, you cycle through several sleep stages two or three times a night, each cycle lasting from 1½ to 3 hours. During the cycle, you move from a light sleep, to a moderately deep sleep, to a deep sleep, back up to a light sleep. This cycle repeats itself.

When you are excited about something, it is fairly common for you to briefly wake up when you reach the top of your sleep cycle. Thus, 3 hours after you have gone to bed, you enter that light phase as the cycle completes itself. At this point, you wake up and immediately start thinking about the competition and worrying about the fact that you are awake. The worry leads to heightened arousal and soon you cannot get back to sleep. Once again, if you could simply accept the temporary waking up, you would quickly go back to sleep.

One aspect of controlling concentration involves teaching yourself to redirect your thoughts in a way that helps you accept these disturbances and prevents you from burning yourself out mentally. You need to learn to direct attention to those thoughts and cues that will optimize performance by raising or lowering arousal as the situation requires. Obviously, you can accomplish this goal in a great many ways. One is to use something going on around you as a focus for your attention. You could occupy yourself with a boring task (e.g., a dull book), something that would keep you from worrying and that would allow you to naturally relax. Ideally, you should not need assistance, but sometimes a little professional help can be valuable. Unfortunately, some athletes never allow anyone else to help them.

If you have a sleeping problem before a major competition or when traveling you are not alone. Many athletes have this problem, and the procedures in this chapter can be of help. Fortunately, the same dedication that helps athletes develop superior sport skills and the mastery of concentration skills can help you conquer any sleeping problems you might have.

I sometimes assist athletes by providing them with a 10-minute casette tape designed to put them to sleep. Most athletes now travel with small tape recorders. All they do is place the tape on their recorder, lie down, turn it on, and go to sleep. Frequently, roommates tell me that the athlete was sound asleep within the first 2 or 3 minutes of the tape.

There is really nothing magical about the tape. All it does is direct athletes' very active minds to the content of the tape, thus preventing them from worrying. They cannot simultaneously concentrate on my instructions on the tape and worry about the competition. Consequently, they quickly relax and fall asleep quite naturally.

The script I use to help athletes go to sleep is given on these pages. If you do have problems sleeping before a competition, you may find it helpful to make your own tape. Simply read the script onto a tape in a slow monotonous voice. Occasionally, athletes will find that their own voice or that of a close friend acts as a distractor. If this is a problem, you can purchase commercial tapes from Enhanced Performance, 12468 Bodega Way, San Diego, CA, 92128. The cost of each tape is $10.00.

This is a tape to help you sleep. What I want you to do is begin by making yourself as comfortable as you possibly can. Lie down where you won't be disturbed. . . . Get into a comfortable position and close your eyes. . . . Just close your eyes. . . and completely relax. . . .

That's fine. . . . Now just let yourself relax and listen to the things that I say. . . . If your mind wanders once in a while . . .that's all right. . .just gently bring it back to the sound of my voice. . . .

You can begin by relaxing all of the muscles in your right arm. . . . Relax all of the muscles in fingers. . .hand. . .wrist . . .forearm. . .and upper arm. . . . That's fine. . . . Now inhale deeply. . .and exhale slowly. . . . As you exhale. . .and relax all of the muscles in your right arm. . .you can feel it become heavier. . . . It is pleasantly heavy. . .drifting down with each breath. . . .

Continue to breath deeply and slowly. . .and now relax all of the muscles in your left arm. . . . In the fingers. . .hand. . . forearm. . .and upper arm. . . . Once again. . .notice as you relax those muscles. . .the pleasant increase in heaviness in your arm as you exhale.

Completely relax all of the muscles in both arms. . .and notice as you exhale the pleasant increase in heaviness as your arms press down against the bed. . . . Completely relaxed . . . . Drifting down. . .toward a very deep. . .comfortable. . . relaxing sleep. . . .

That's fine. . .now relax all of the muscles in your right leg
. . . . Relax the muscles in the foot. . .ankle. . .calf. . .and thigh.
Just completely relax. . .let yourself go. . .enjoy the pleasant
feelings of relaxation. . . . With each breath feeling your body
drift down. . .into a deep. . .relaxing sleep. . . .

Relax all of the muscles in your left leg. . . . Relax the muscles
in the foot. . .ankle. . .calf. . .and thigh. . . . Completely relaxed
. . .drifting down into a very comfortable. . .deep. . .relaxing
sleep. . . . Relaxing all of the muscles in both arms. . .and both
legs. . . . Very comfortable. . . . Completely relaxed. . . .

Relax the muscles in your face. . . . In your forehead. . .and
around your eyes. . . . Relax the muscles in your jaw. . . . Just
let your mouth open slightly. . . . Completely relaxed. . . . With
each breath drifting down. . . . down. . . . down. . .into a deep
. . .comfortable. . .sleep.

Now. . .I am going to count from 1 to 20. . . . With each count
. . .you will find yourself drifting down. . .deeper. . .and deeper
. . . . Into a very relaxed. . .deep sleep. . . . You will drift down
. . . . deeper. . .and deeper into a very comfortable. . .sleep. . . .
When you wake up you will feel refreshed. . . and confident
. . . . knowing that you will be able to perform up to your full
potential. . . .

One. . . . drifting down. . . . deeper. . .and deeper. . . . into
a very relaxed. . .comfortable. . .sleep. . . . Two. . . . down. . . .
down. . . . down. . . . completely relaxed. . . . drifting. . . floating
. . . . deeper. . . . deeper. . . . still deeper. . . . Three . . . . Four
. . . with each count drifting down. . . . with each breath becoming more and more relaxed. . .more and more deeply
asleep. . . .

Five. . .relaxing all of the muscles in both arms. . .and both
legs. . . . completely relaxed. . .drifting down. . .deeper. . .and
deeper. . .deeper. . .and deeper. Six. . .down. . . . down. . . .
down. . . . Seven. . . . Eight. . .deep asleep. . . completely relaxed
. . . drifting. . .floating. . . . Nine. . .down. . .down. . .down. . . .

Ten. . .with each count drifting down deeper and deeper. . . .
knowing that when you wake up you will feel refreshed. . .and
confident. . . . Eleven. . .with each breath drifting down. . .into
a very deep. . .comfortable. . .relaxing sleep. . . . down. . . .
down. . . . down. . . .

Twelve. . .drifting. . .down. . .deeper. . .and deeper. . . . Thir-
teen. . . . Fourteen. . . . Fifteen. . . . deeper and deeper. . . .
deeper and deeper. . . . Sixteen. . .completely relaxed. . . . deep
asleep. . . . deep asleep. . . .

Seventeen. . .drifting. . .down. . .deeper. . .and deeper. . .still
deeper. . . . down. . . . down. . . . Eighteen. . . . Nineteen. . . .
Twenty. . . . deep asleep. . .knowing that when you wake up
. . . . You'll feel refreshed. . . .confident. . . .able to perform up
to your potential. . . .

SUMMARY

Chapter 8 explains how to direct attention to those thoughts and cues which will optimize performance by lowering arousal as the situation requires.

Sleeplessness before an important competition is a very common problem with many athletes. It can be alleviated if the following points are kept in mind:

1. Each of us has an identifiable sleep cycle during which we move from light to medium to heavy sleep.

2. Prior to a competition, experienced athletes find themselves with excess energy and time on hand because there is a lighter period of training at this stage. Consequently, they are not fatigued enough!

3. When their normal sleep pattern is disturbed, they start to worry and burn up valuable emotional and physical energy. The worry over not sleeping has created the problem, not the lack of sleep.

4. Learning to distract themselves with a boring task or a relaxation tape can keep athletes from worrying and thereby allow them to relax naturally.

Chapter 9 will show techniques that can be helpful in focusing attention as a means to maintaining concentration under pressure.

9

Centering

Centering, or focusing attention on the "one point" as it is described by some martial arts experts, is a means of maintaining control over tension and concentration under pressure. As a process, centering involves learning to direct your thoughts toward the *center of gravity* in your own body. The center of gravity is a point just behind your navel. According to practitioners of aikido, when you are able to "let your mind rest" on this point, you are centered. The feeling of being centered is a strong, confident, anchored kind of feeling. The best way to describe it is by getting you to experience a certain feeling now, and to then relate this feeling to a couple of common sport situations.

As you read this book, I want you to begin to pay attention to your breathing. Take three or four deep breaths and carefully observe what happens to your body in relation to the chair in which you are sitting. Do this now.

Did you notice that on the inhale you seemed to increase tension in your upper body, and to almost rise up a little? On the exhale, you should have felt yourself sinking down, becoming heavier, making more solid contact with the chair. If you did not, try again; only this time do two things: First, inhale deeply from your abdomen, not from your chest; secondly, as you exhale, consciously relax the muscles in your buttocks, thighs, and calves.

Now, try the same thing again, but this time take four breaths. I want to complicate it just a little, though. In your own mind, come up with a number—it does not matter what the number is—that represents to you how heavy you feel against the chair. For example, I might give myself a 5 right now before inhaling or exhaling. Your task as you inhale is to make sure that you do not become any lighter. Do not raise yourself up, going from a 5 to a 3 for example. Then, as you exhale, you want to feel yourself relax even more, becoming heavier and more centered. Thus, I might stay at a 5 on the first inhale and drop to a 7 on the first exhale. With breath 2, my goal is to remain at 7 on the inhale, and to drop even further on the exhale. With breath 3, I want to become even more centered on the exhale. Go ahead and try this now.

Think about some sport situations. Can you recall times when you felt centered, when you had the kind of steady anchored feeling that you just experienced? Perhaps you were at the free-throw line in a basketball game and you really felt comfortable. You knew before you released the ball that it was going in the basket. You might have noticed a similar feeling in golf or tennis. In golf you felt "grounded" and solid as you addressed the ball. In tennis you knew as you started your serve that it was going in. That centered feeling can be contrasted to the unsteady, out-of-balance feeling you have when you are slightly anxious, feeling out of balance, like a triangle that is standing on a point instead of on its base. For example, in basketball you cannot seem to get your feet in the right position at the free-throw line. You feel you are working hard but do not achieve the desired result. Though you push the ball toward the basket, it does not seem to go as far as it should, given the effort. The movements themselves were quick, but it seemed as if you were pushing air and the ball just did not travel as far as it should have.

Gymnasts and divers can quickly associate with the feeling of being centered. Divers on the board, or gymnasts on the balance beam, when confident, feel steady and anchored. They are making good contact with the board or beam which perceptually seems quite wide. Raise the elevation of the apparatus or increase the difficulty of the task, and suddenly the beam seems very narrow. When they were anchored, there were no thoughts of falling off. Now, with increasing tension in the upper body, due to breathing changes associated with the pressure, they feel unsteady and they are! To make matters worse, thoughts about falling lead to actual body movements which result in mistakes. Test yourself on that. Try walking along a line or along the curb of a sidewalk. Notice that a fear about leaning too far to one side almost always results in your compensating by leaning in the opposite direction. Suddenly, you are seesawing back and forth, trying to regain your balance.

It does not matter if you are a football player trying to block an opponent or a gymnast on a balance beam; the feeling of being centered not only generates confidence, but positively affects strength, coordination, and timing. A pass blocker who is off balance in football is going to be beaten.

Centering is not mystical but has a rational explanation. Optimal performance requires an appropriate level of physical arousal and an appropriate attentional focus. The process of centering involves directing your thoughts internally for a moment to mentally check and to adjust your breathing and level of muscle tension. In this way, you consciously counteract any involuntary changes that may have occurred because of pressure in the competitive situation. Thus, if you had started to hyperventilate, which means breathing rapidly up in your chest, the centering process would allow you to become aware of this and to change it. It is critical that you learn to make these adjustments. Left unchecked, small changes in breathing will lead to excessive muscle tension, especially in antagonistic muscles, and will interfere with coordination and timing.

The reason that breathing and muscle tension get out of control in sports activities is that most of us do not take the time to pay attention to our bodies. Under pressure, we stop thinking. As a result, we become aware of the tension only after it is too late, after it has already affected performance.

There is an additional, very important reason for taking the time to mentally check and to adjust your breathing and muscle tension. The *conscious* effort of attending to breathing has a secondary effect. You cannot simultaneously, consciously attend to both breathing and worry. Thus, in conjunction with an adjustment in tension comes a mental clearing. For the moment you have gotten rid of any negative or tension-inducing thoughts. This places you in a position to be able to direct attention and concentration to the most task-relevant cues. Now, you can decide what it is that you need to attend to.

All you are trying to accomplish by centering is that momentary clearing and readjustment which maximizes the likelihood that you will be able to zero in on task-relevant cues. In effect, you are providing a base from which to initiate activity. It is the development of this base that will lead to consistency in performance. If you always start at the same place, you are much more likely to be consistent whether you are swinging a golf club, a tennis racquet, or approaching a high-jump bar.

The actual process of centering is as simple as the process you just went through. With some practice, it can be confined to a single breath. In the time it takes to inhale and exhale once from down in your abdomen, you can adjust tension level, clear your thoughts, and be in a position of control, deciding what you will attend to. You are no longer controlled by your own anxiety or distracted by task-irrelevant cues.

Although you can center from any position, it is helpful to learn to center from a standing position for two reasons: First, most competitive situations involve a standing position; second, this position is more difficult to control. Thus, you have more to gain by learning to center while standing.

I ask people to begin by standing with their feet about shoulder-distance apart and one foot slightly in front of the other. This position is preferred because it is more balanced than many other standing positions. It is more difficult to push you off balance when you are standing in this manner.

Next, check to make sure that your knees are slightly bent. This is critical. To feel the increase in heaviness that occurs, you need to feel the changes taking place in muscles in your calves and thighs. If you knees are locked they will prevent you from perceiving these changes. Locked knees are one of the reasons many athletes cannot tell if they are relaxed in a competitive situation or not. Athletes who lock their knees prior to beginning their performance are covering up an important cue for assessing their level of arousal.

Now, when you inhale deeply, do so from your abdomen. On the inhale mentally check the tension in your chest, neck, and shoulder muscles and consciously let them relax. As you exhale, relax the muscles in your calves and thighs. Let your knees bend slightly and your hips drop lower. As you do this, you should feel the increased heaviness and contact that your body is making with the ground. It is at the end of this breath that you will be ready to redirect attention to the task or competitive situation.

As you can see, the process of centering is very simple. What is difficult is remembering to center, being able to center under pressure, knowing when to center, and most importantly, knowing what to attend to after having centered.

WHEN DO YOU CENTER?

As described here, centering is a conscious process and not something that you do automatically. It cannot be because it is designed to get you to use conscious thoughts in order to avoid losing control. Because centering is a conscious process (you actively think about it while doing it), you cannot center when you must be actively attending to something else. *Notice*, I did not say you cannot center while performing. You can! If performance is automatic (not requiring conscious thought), you can center even while performing.

The conscious process of centering is designed to improve your performance. Thus, you do not need to center in those situations where you feel confident and are in control. Instead, when you are having difficulties, when confidence is low, when performance expectancies are high, when you are frustrated, angry, worried, or anxious, you want to use your centering skills.

Test yourself *when* performance problems are most likely to develop in your sport:

1. When are you most likely to make attentional errors?

   _____
   _____
   _____

2. When are you most likely to be too tense and tight?

   _____
   _____
   _____

3. When are you most likely to become too relaxed?

   _____
   _____
   _____

Obviously, there are individual differences in terms of the types of situations that will be stressful. Some athletes have problems under highly specific conditions. For example, a hitter may not be able to hit a particular pitcher or a pitcher cannot pitch to a particular hitter.

In addition to specific times when each athlete will want to center, there are some general times when almost all athletes will find it useful to center. For example, I recommend always centering just before beginning any competitive event because it helps alleviate precontest anxiety. I also recommend that you center as you are about to end the contest. Often, the last attempt during the last few seconds or minutes of the game is sloppy, especially when the outcome is still in doubt. Increasing arousal at this time is likely to interfere with both concentration and physical tension. Other generally stressful times would include any "must situations": You must sink the putt, you must win the point, you must score on this possession, and so on.

Finally, I recommend you center in between performance sequences in sports like gymnastics and skating. Both of these sports have "transition points" pauses, (e.g., just prior to a tumbling run in gymnastics or the "setting up time" between jumps in skating) where there is time to let your thoughts go inward momentarily to check your breathing, and to adjust your muscle tension.

Remember, centering at the start of an activity can provide the foundation or base that will allow for consistency and improved coordination and timing. Imagine a high jumper making an approach to the high-jump bar. Just before jumping, he or she must plant his or her take-off leg. At this point, the jumper lowers his or her hips and drops down. Remember, to get up and over the bar, a jumper must first bend the knee and lower the body so he or she can use his or her leg strength. If breathing is off even slightly, the jumper may inhale while trying to drop down. This insignificant action can reduce the jumper's ability to get as low as needed, especially if his or her breathing has also resulted in a tightening of muscles in the chest, neck, and shoulders.

Imagine yourself taking off in an attempt to clear the bar in the high jump. What would happen to your effort if you exhaled at the same time you were trying to reach up and over the bar? Would you not be working against yourself? Imagine suddenly feeling the heaviness you feel when you center (exhale), when you are trying to jump up. The coordination of breathing to effort is absolutely critical. Under normal conditions you do not have to think about it. In fact, if you have to think about your breathing during the attempt, you are in trouble. Instead, you need to create the conditions prior to the jump so that breathing, muscle tension, and concentration are likely to be synchronized. In the high jump, this occurs at the start of the approach. In golf, it occurs at the start of the swing. In skating, it may occur several times between jumps. To help you make a decision about when to center, follow these two rules:

1. You must have the opportunity to direct your concentration inward, momentarily to adjust breathing and muscle tension.
2. You must time the centering process so that it occurs as closely as possible to the point in time when you actually begin a motor sequence (e.g., the approach in the high jump or the take-off for a jump in skating).

The reason the act of centering must occur immediately prior to taking any action is that any delays between centering and performing simply provide the opportunity for new distractions and/or for tension to build up again. Remember, centering is simply a brief time out that gives you momentary control over concentration and tension. To remain in control after centering, you must quickly get involved in the activity. Then, as you have time to think while actually performing (e.g., as between jumps in skating) and as the pressure builds, so, too, does the need to center again.

In sports where the start of activity is under your control, it is fairly easy to time centering to occur just as you are ready to perform. It is a little more difficult in other sports (e.g., boxing). You may have to limit centering to a few key times (e.g., on breaks in boxing or when you are out of the opponent's reach). Appendix A provides you with ideas about when to center and what to attend to in different sports.

CENTERING UNDER PRESSURE

Many individuals find it difficult to remember and to successfully complete a centering procedure under stressful conditions. To be able to take advantage of centering, you must practice just as you would any physical skill. You have to overlearn it in the sense of drilling yourself enough so that you remember to use it. It is helpful to mentally rehearse the centering process. You should take time each day to sit down and visualize the problem situation and the act of centering and coping with that problem. Of course, you should also practice the centering procedure when you actually practice the sport and when you compete.

HAVING CENTERED, TO WHAT DO YOU ATTEND?

Once you have adjusted tension levels and cleared your mind, to what do you direct your attention? Obviously, that depends to a certain extent on your level of skill and on your goals. Unfortunately, there are more wrong things to attend to than right ones. Do not overcomplicate matters, especially during performance. A good question to ask is, "What single cue will help me get involved in the competitive situation and put me on 'automatic pilot'?" Is there a single thought or action that needs to be attended to? What cue will tell you that you are ready? For Tom Petranoff, centering led to awareness of a pounding heart which told him he was ready. Then attention was directed to taking the first step in his approach. After that, everything else was programmed.

You may want to review chapter 5 about what to attend to and what to avoid. In addition, specific programs using centering to control negative thoughts and to speed learning are presented in chapters 11 and 12. These chapters will provide you with ideas regarding the direction of attention.

To shift from a centered position to "focusing your ki," you obviously have to have some target, usually outside of yourself, on which you are concentrating. That target may be the thrower's "hole in the sky" or it may be the karate expert's "point," which is located just a couple of inches in back of the boards or bricks he or she will attempt to break.

To shift from a centered position to a broad-external focus and to increased awareness of surroundings, you must retain your relaxed but attentive state. Thus, as you exhale, you relax the muscles in your calves and thighs; this should allow you to feel yourself centering and to become aware of the increased heaviness as your body presses down against the ground. Once that feeling occurs, you mentally remind yourself to "now pay attention to the environment." You "scan" by moving your eyes looking for "keys" or movements that let you anticipate what will happen. These movements (e.g., an opponent's jab) will trigger an automatic response in you, because you have practiced reacting to them, until they have become "instinctive." Centering has just helped you make sure that you are able to see the things going on so that you will react.

Centering can be used to help you develop that broad-external focus associated with *assessing* the environment, as above, and it can be used as the jumping-off point for *narrowing* attention. Likewise, many athletes use centering as a brief time-out procedure to remind themselves to slow down and *prepare*, and/or *analyze* before reacting. You probably have had several instances where you found yourself pressured to respond before you were ready. Golfers who let a foursome behind them pressure them into rushing a shot are an example. By teaching yourself to become more aware of your increasing pressure (e.g., by being sensitive to muscle tension changes in your body), you can learn to avoid rushing. As pressure and tension build, those physical sensations become the signal to you to center, to take time out to calm yourself, and to adequately prepare (e.g., by mentally rehearsing your shot and by adjusting tension). Here the awareness of stress is the signal to center; the self-instruction that follows directs your attention to the cues that tell you if you can call a temporary halt to the action in order to gain more time to prepare.

One of the things I teach Olympic athletes is to automatically react to any unforeseen or unexpected happening by centering and then shifting to an assessment focus. Once the situation has been assessed, they can competently decide how best to respond. Taking the time to center can keep you from being pushed into an action before you are ready. It is the kind of process a good professional witness goes through before answering an attorney's questions during cross-examination.

SUMMARY

Chapter 9 explains the concept of centering, a quick technique you can use to momentarily gain control over the physical tension and mental distractions which keep you from concentrating effectively.

In order to be successful with centering you have to remember the following points:

1. You have to be in a situation that allows you to momentarily direct your thoughts internally.
2. You can center while performing provided the performance is either so highly developed that it is automatic, or so simple that you can split concentration.
3. You are most likely to need to center immediately *prior to beginning* an activity, *during lulls* in a competition, and *just before the last few moments* of a tight game.
4. Following the process of centering, it is very important to have something specific to which to direct attention immediately and to get involved in performance.

Chapter 10 will demonstrate how athletes can train themselves to center successfully and focus attention in the most effective way.

10

Testing Your Ability to Center and to Focus Attention

Just as a diver left the 10-meter tower to execute a difficult dive, another diver jumped off beside him and started carrying on a conversation as they were falling through the air. This was just one of the little games that athletes played with each other to see if they could maintain the narrow focus of attention required by divers. Football coaches attempt to teach their players to maintain a broad-external focus of attention, which is often necessary in football, by placing them in the center of a circle of would-be blockers. Each player who makes up the circle has a number and when his number is called he charges in, trying to hit the player in the center. If the player fails to be aware and sensitive to the entire circle, he will be knocked down by the blocker because he will be hit from the side or from behind.

In aikido, our instructor would test our ability to center by having us kneel quietly on the mats in the dojo. We would sit back on our heels with our backs straight and our eyes closed. We would be told that if we centered properly, we would be immovable. We knelt in this position long enough for the blood flow to be restricted from our feet so that we were in some pain and it was difficult to concentrate on our breathing and the one point. Only then would our instructor begin his test. He would sneak about the mat quietly enough so that we would hear an occasional sound but not know for sure where he was. As a result, our concentration was further disturbed by our attempts to locate him. Suddenly he would run into one of us, toppling us over. Then in anger he would shout we were not concentrating. Like the divers, our instructor was testing our ability to center under adverse conditions. Our anxiety and concern about him and about what he would do kept our attention split. Trying to anticipate and plan for his attacks, we would brace by tightening up muscles and lean to meet his attack. It was a simple matter for him to use our lean against us and pull us off balance.

For most of us, attempting to test our concentration under the conditions imposed by a group of divers, or by my aikido instructor, is a little premature. First, we need to test ourselves under less stressful conditions. Then, as we begin to have some success and our confidence builds, we can increase the pressure. It is important for you to challenge yourself—to see that you are gaining control over both arousal and concentration.

Fortunately, you can do some exercises from the martial arts to test your ability to center and to direct the flow of energy or ki. The first exercise involves using the centering procedure to lower your own center of gravity enough so that two strong individuals cannot lift you off the ground (Figure 10.1).

To try the lifting test, stand with your feet about shoulder distance apart, one slightly in front of the other. You should

FIGURE 10.1 The lifting test is a concentration exercise you can master with practice.

have a slight bend in your knees and the muscles in your legs should be relaxed. Your arms should be extended down toward the floor. They will be located about 4 to 8 inches away from your sides, and it should feel to you as if they are being pulled down toward the ground so hard that they are stiff and unbendable, like an iron bar.

The individuals who are to lift you should be standing on either side of you. When you are ready, have each of them grab one of your arms at the wrist as they would hold a baseball bat. The one on the right will have your right arm and the one on the left will be holding your left arm.

Now, the first time that you ask them to lift you, see if you can help them by thinking *up*. Let your eyes roll up to look up, inhale by breathing up in your chest. Let your body straighten up and think about being picked up. Do not jump off the ground, just let your inhalation straighten you up, making you lighter and easier to lift. As you are breathing in, have them lift. If they are bigger and taller than you and stronger, they should have little trouble getting you off the ground.

Once they have lifted you, it is time to use your centering ability to prevent them from getting you off the ground a second time. To do this, assume the same starting position as before. Now, with your arms extended downward and your knees slightly bent, inhale deeply from your abdomen. As you inhale make sure you do not increase the muscle tension in your chest, neck, or shoulders. While you exhale, make sure the muscles in your legs are relaxed and your knees bend just slightly. You should feel yourself sinking down, becoming heavier and centered. Let your thoughts focus on this feeling of heaviness in your lower body and at the end of the breath when you are at your heaviest, nod to signal them that they are to lift you.

If you are concentrating on the feelings of heaviness and keeping the muscles in your lower body relaxed, they will not be able to lift you off the floor. By concentrating as described, you will have lowered your center of gravity slightly. In addition, although your arms are extended stiffly at your sides, they are not, or should not be braced. In other words, you are tensing your extensor muscles as you think of your arms extending through the floor; you are *not* tensing flexor muscles (your biceps). It also means that the muscles in your

shoulders, which are used to elevate the shoulders, are relaxed. This has the effect that the person on each side will
try to lift by pushing your shoulders up against your neck.
The result is they will be pushing against each other rather
than being able to coordinate their effort. The way to breathe
and think has dramatically altered your center of gravity and
other people's ability to lift you or to push you off balance.

You will probably find that as you learn to center, your ability to keep yourself from being lifted improves. At first, you
may only be able to increase the degree of difficulty the two
people have in lifting you. Often, there is some initial success,
but as soon as the lifters begin to strain a little and you feel
a slight wobble, concentration is broken. That famous "oh
no" thought comes in, you catch your breath (breathing up
in your chest) and momentarily brace, and you are suddenly
picked up off the floor. As you get better at concentrating, you
will find you can have those momentary lapses, giving the
lifters the feeling that they are about to be successful, and yet
still regain your concentration quickly enough to recenter,
stopping any further lifting.

To test your ability to "focus your ki," to get all of your
strength and energy channeled in one direction, try the
unbendable arm exercise (Figure 10.2). To do this, find someone who is big and strong and tell him or her that you want
to see if you can keep your arm from being bent. Make sure,
however, that the person will cooperate and wait for your
instructions.

Take your preferred arm and, with the person facing you,
extend your arm out and over his or her shoulder. If you are
right handed, your right arm will be extended out, palm up,
over the person's left shoulder. The wrist of your right arm
should be resting on the person's shoulder and you should
have a very slight bend in your arm at the elbow.

The person who is trying to bend your arm should reach
up with both hands, and interlock his or her fingers, letting
the hands come to rest on your arm at the elbow joint. When
you say "ready," the person should apply pressure with both
hands, pulling down in an attempt to bend your arm.

If you begin to brace (tensing flexor muscles) in response
to the challenge to bend your arm, you will work against
yourself. The excitement of the challenge can cause you to

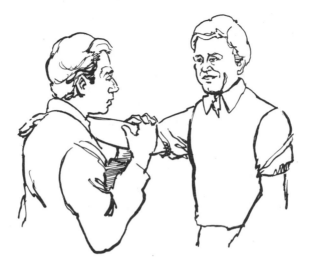

FIGURE 10.2 Here is another concentration exercise you can practice.

flex your biceps muscles which bend your arm. Thus, even though you are using extensor muscles to resist, your excessive arousal results in the biceps working against you. You have not been successful in "focusing your ki" if this happens.

To avoid bracing and to develop the right mental attitude, begin with a small bend in your arm at the elbow. Then, when you are ready, after having centered, you want to redirect your thoughts toward thinking of a force that is pouring out of your extended arm. Signal them to begin trying to bend your arm, but keep your concentration focused on that force. As you concentrate on the force, you will feel your arm begin to extend out. The bend in your elbow will become smaller as that extension occurs. This feeling will let you know that you are relaxing the biceps and using your extensor muscles. So long as you sustain this concentration, the person will not be able to bend your arm. You have not changed the available strength in your body or your body mass. Learning to center and concentrate has not given you more power, weight, or strength; it simply helped you use what you have.

Under normal conditions, you believe that two strong people should be able to lift you. As a result, when presented with the challenge to keep them from lifting you, your self-doubt causes you to tighten up, involuntarily doing the precise things to your body that will help them lift you. Your thoughts served as attentional distractors that affected physiology in a negative way as far as performance is concerned. By centering and redirecting concentration, you can prevent this from happening.

Challenging others to lift you, or to bend your arm, can be a fun way to test your ability to center and to focus your concentration. It can also help to build confidence in yourself, and in your ability to use these techniques. Now you must measure success in actual competitive conditions. You need to begin to build mental skills such as centering and attentional redirection into the actual competitive situation. The next two chapters will help you accomplish this.

SUMMARY

Chapter 10 describes two exercises which test an athlete's ability to center under adverse conditions and which can ultimately improve control over both arousal and concentration:

1. The *lifting-up* exercise uses the mental procedure of centering to lower an athlete's own center of gravity enough so that two strong individuals cannot lift him or her off the ground.

2. The *unbendable arm* exercise teaches the athlete to "focus ki" by channeling all the strength and energy in one direction.

The next chapters will help you build mental skills such as centering and attentional redirection for actual competitive situations.

11

Centering and Mental Rehearsal

Most highly skilled athletes strive to achieve that level of performance where everything is automatic. The more complex the sport, the longer it takes to achieve that automatic level. With enough practice, skills like diving and typing become highly automated.

Recall from chapter 9 that athletes need to be aware of two broad focuses of attention: (a) a *broad-internal* attention which you use to analyze and plan, and (b) a *broad-external type* of attention which you use to rapidly assess situations. In fact, some analysis takes place with both types of attention. With the internal type of attention, analysis is a very systematic process. You are asking and answering a series of your own questions at a conscious level. The speed of that analysis is much slower than the type of "intuitive" analysis that occurs when you react in an unconscious or automatic way.

The broad-external "mind like water" type of attention is the type of concentration employed when analysis occurs at an intuitive level. Typically, conscious thought involving a series of questions or an inner dialogue is nonexistent. Because the situation you are assessing is so familiar, like following the flight of a ball in baseball or tennis, the normal series of questions leading to a decision are bypassed. Instead, your mind leaps from the stimulus directly to a conclusion (e.g., a decision about when to swing).

Obviously, the athlete who can shorten the analytical process and still anticipate the course of action or outcome has a decided edge over the athlete who must stop and think. It is the overlearning of performance sequences which allows you to develop these automatic responses. Constant exposure to situations and the repeated response to those situations will let you perform at what appears to be an automatic level.

Unfortunately, several things slow down our learning and keep us from automating responses as quickly as we might like:

1. We cannot actually perform in the situation as much as we would like. We do not get enough opportunities to play or compete.

2. Anxiety and pressure increase the noise in our learning system and prevent us from controlling tension and concentrating as we should. We attend to and practice the wrong things, building up competing responses.

3. When we are trying to correct mistakes, we often focus on the wrong things. We attempt to change the result or symptom rather than the cause.

4. The performance itself is so demanding that it does not allow us to practice various elements in isolation. We must put everything together all at once to be successful.

Relaxation and mental rehearsal can provide a partial solution to points 1 and 2, especially when you rehearse the activity from the perspective of the performer and emphasize the actual motor sequence and emotional state. Even though you might not be able to practice a shot as often as you would like, or to find yourself in a particular competitive situation very frequently, you can mentally rehearse those conditions. How you rehearse, however, is critical, especially if you hope to overcome points 3 and 4 as well.

I have spoken about the importance of transition points, those points in a motor sequence where your body changes directions (e.g., top of the back swing in golf, the takeoff from a jump). Chances are if you close your eyes and mentally rehearse from inside your own body any sport sequence, you will be able to quickly identify the transition points. You will tend to rehearse the activity in natural segments. The breaking points between segments are transition points. It is at these transition points where you typically receive feedback telling you if everything is all right.

When you drive home from a familiar place and are preoccupied with something inside your head, you pass through many transition points without being aware of them. You changed lanes, made turns, reacted to drivers merging into your lane, stopped at lights and stop signs, slowed for intersections, and so on. At each of these transition points, you were attending to external cues while you were actively processing and analyzing other events internally. As long as the feedback you received from the environment was within "normal limits," it did not require conscious attention for you to react and to respond. Thus, at each transition point, things were progressing normally, and you did not receive negative feedback. If a car had suddenly swerved or braked, you would have reacted. The unusual or irregular cue would have disturbed your internal processing and forced you to consciously attend to what was going on around you in order to choose a course of action.

Performance in a sport situation can be similar to putting the car on automatic pilot. For this to occur, however, each of these transitions must be smooth; negative feedback cannot occur. By continually rehearsing these transitions, you can learn to groove them to the point that adjustments become automatic. Even more important, mental rehearsal, when it involves feelings as well as images, can help develop consistency and stabilize your performance. By using centering to provide a constant base (e.g., consistent level of tension and concentration at the start of a performance sequence), and by rehearsing and mentally practicing the activity, you can speed learning and increase consistency.

If you think about it, you will realize that the "funny feeling" you get during a transition, which tells you something is not quite right, is a result of something being wrong earlier in the performance sequence. For example, a high jumper who becomes aware at the transition between his approach and his takeoff that he is leaning into the bar may attempt a correction during the jump. Sometimes, he will be successful. The lean that the athlete is correcting, however, began before he ever reached the transition point. Too often, we do not become sensitive to problems until transition points occur.

Then, many athletes have a tendency to alter something at the transition point itself, rather than changing the conditions that led to the problem in the first place. Through a careful analysis of the entire motor sequence, you can detect the beginning of the error, and by altering things at the beginning, prevent the symptom entirely.

MENTAL REHEARSAL TO AID IN LOCATING PROBLEMS

You can detect problems in your own performance sooner and make the necessary corrections by using the information presented above. When you find you are having difficulty, take the time to list all the transition points in the particular performance situation. Next, try and locate the first point where you became aware of the problem. That is, when did you begin to get some visual or auditory feedback telling you things were not going as planned? Once you have located this point, begin tracing back along the various performance segments to see where the problem might have started. For example, tennis players who hit their volley long when running to the net may not have become aware of a problem until they saw the ball go out, or until they felt the contact between the racquet and ball, realizing they had not compensated for their forward motion. To correct the problem, they might change their body position when they first begin their movement to the net. In a similar way, golfers who realize that they have a problem at the point of impact may find the problem began when the back swing was first started. The correction needs to take place there.

CENTERING AND REHEARSAL

When athletes are learning new skills or refining existing ones, I have them combine the use of centering procedures with a more complete *mental rehearsal process*. Some sport psychologists prefer going through an extensive relaxation procedure to reduce anxiety prior to the rehearsal process. My feeling is that this is not necessary with many athletes.

In fact, most can learn to rehearse an entire sequence with their eyes open while engaging in some other, automatic activity.

I remember hearing Britain's National Rowing coach talking about how badly she wanted to include psychological training in the British program, but lamenting that the athletes had no time in their schedules for another activity. She pointed out they were up early for a practice before having to drive 1½ hours in London traffic to get to work. They then worked all day and drove another 1½ hours in heavy traffic for another workout and a meal. It was all they could do after this to just go to bed. She had not entertained the notion that much of the rehearsal and mental work in which the athlete would be engaging should be occurring during practice. It is during practice that you should be practicing concentration and tension control. Likewise, this coach had not considered the fact that in stop-and-go traffic, there are many opportunities to think of and to rehearse other things besides how irritated you are with the drivers around you and with the delays. Being able to find times to rehearse while you are away from the actual competition is a desirable goal.

When I first start teaching athletes to rehearse, I have them sit down someplace where they will not be disturbed. Usually, I ask them to close their eyes, at least for the first couple of times. I explain to them that the goal of the rehearsal process is to anticipate various competitive situations and skills and to practice these until they become automatic. At first, rehearsal will not be in real time. Instead, they will slow their thought process for each of the transition points and take their time making the connections. Gymnasts or divers may go through this type of process to teach themselves to feel and to visualize what a dive will be like before they ever attempt it.

I always ask athletes to begin the rehearsal process by building in centering as a means of making sure they start at an appropriate level of arousal and with an awareness of their tension level. They are instructed to time the centering to end as closely to the start of the sport activity as possible.

Using sprinters as an example, I have them sit down and close their eyes. Then they begin to visualize themselves in the race situation. They are looking out of their own body. The sprinters see the other competitors, the starting blocks, officials, and so on. Then they hear the call to take their mark, see themselves move into the blocks, and as they kneel down, visualize and feel the entire process of positioning their hands on the track and reaching back for the blocks with their feet. As the sprinters get into position, but before they react to the call to "get set," they mentally rehearse taking that centering breath. They actually inhale while rehearsing and, on the inhale, relax the neck and shoulder muscles. On the exhale, they relax leg muscles and feel themselves settle into the blocks.

At the end of that breath, they move up into the "set" position and direct their attention to the starter. Next, they rehearse the start by waiting for the gun and then exploding out of the blocks. At first, they very carefully rehearse every detail of that start. They feel the drive of their arms and legs and mentally rehearse each step, lengthening their stride and beginning to straighten up they move down the track. Midway through the race, they mentally check the tension in their upper body and, if necessary, adjust it, relaxing neck and shoulder muscles. As the race continues, the athletes become aware of their feelings at the three-quarter mark. If they have an instruction that they want to give to themselves at this point in the race, or something that they want to direct their attention to (e.g., "relax," "lean for the tape"), they would rehearse it. Finally, they rehearse the finish and follow through, those few steps down the track beyond the finish.

The transition points, because of their complexity, have to be emphasized early and rehearsed slowly as the athletes carefully analyze and check what they are feeling at each of these critical times. Then, as they become more comfortable, rehearsal can be speeded up so that it eventually occurs in real time, the length of time it takes to actually run the race.

Obviously, there are some exceptions to real time rehearsal. A marathon runner would have to spend a very long time rehearsing a race! When the event is this lengthy, select segments or parts where the rehearsal process is more critical because you need to emphasize a transition, the development of an attitude, or an ability to respond at a particular time in the competition (to an opponent's surge, for example).

With some athletes, as the rehearsal process becomes smoother, I add music as a means of helping them get a better feeling of the exact time the event takes and as a means of increasing confidence. Thus, sprinters use a particular piece of music, which they mentally rehearse, to help them time their stride.

To illustrate the rehearsal process in a team sport, imagine playing basketball: You have the ball, and you are leading a fast break. There are three of you and two defensive players. You are dribbling up the middle, and you have a teammate on either side.

Now, let us move this situation back in time. You are on defense, and you see your center controlling a rebound. At this point your rehearsal begins. You use your next breath as a centering breath. On the inhale, you mentally check neck and shoulder muscle tension. As you begin to exhale, you are already moving down the floor. Quickly you direct attention backward for the outlet pass. You follow the ball into your hands, turn and dribble. You are aware of each stride and of each bounce of the ball. Now, you reach a point where the defensive players must commit themselves. Just before hitting that point, you quickly check the positions of your teammates.

Initially, as the defense commits the rehearsal slows down. You carefully examine in slow motion the cues telling you whether to pass, to drive for the basket, or to stop short and take a jump shot. You imagine the moves the defense would make, which will dictate each of your moves, and you systematically rehearse your responses. As you become more and more sensitive to these defensive moves, you begin speeding up the rehearsal process until it occurs in real time.

Ultimately, the goal of this rehearsal is to reach the point where you can rehearse an entire sequence, in real time, with your eyes open, while you are engaged in some other activity such as walking down the street, riding on a bus, and so on.

I cannot overemphasize how important this type of rehearsal is. It leads to greater anticipation and to overlearning, which will prevent performance from being disrupted by anxiety and pressure. This type of rehearsal can help you keep your timing sharp even when you are injured. Thus, although you may not be able to put all of the physical pressure on yourself because a knee or elbow will not take it, you can mentally keep the timing sharp and the motor responses grooved.

SUMMARY

Chapter 11 outlines the use of the rehearsal process in actual competitive situations:

1. The goal is to increase your ability to anticipate and to react at an automatic level and to speed the learning process.
2. You should incorporate the centering process into the rehearsal. This will help you monitor tension levels and adjust them, in practice as well as in competition. Without an awareness of your own feelings, you cannot make corrections.
3. Centering allows you to create the conditions at the start of a performance sequence that will let you control both arousal and focus of concentration.
4. You need to begin by allowing yourself to emphasize the transition points between motor segments. Slow down the rehearsal process until you thoroughly understand and have complete control over these transitions. This means you have a total awareness of what you should feel, see, and hear as you move through this part of the performance.
5. Slowly move toward rehearsing the entire sequence in real time. Depending upon how complex the activity, this may take only a few, or hundreds of repetitions.

Chapter 12 will help athletes control distractions and negative feelings during competitions.

12

Controlling Distractions and Negative Thoughts

Although automatic performance is a decided asset in most situations, you now face a new type of problem—too much time to think!

Like the driver of a car who can think while driving, an athlete whose performance is automatic can also think of other things while performing. If these thoughts are anxiety-inducing, or lead to self-doubt, performance can deteriorate rapidly.

Bruce Ogilvie, one of the founding fathers of applied sport psychology in the United States, tells a story illustrating the problems that can occur when you have too much time to think. He also illustrates one of the ways to cope with this problem.

Dr. Ogilvie was watching a group of receivers run out for passes at a rookie training camp in the National Football League. As he described it, the athletes were all extremely talented with great speed and great hands. Yet, as they were running out for passes, their anxiety and concern over making the team was getting to them. Instead of performing at the level at which they were capable, they were frequently dropping passes.

It seemed as if each mistake or each dropped pass only made the situation worse. Dr. Ogilvie could see the athletes physically tightening up, especially in their hands. While the athletes were running pass routes, they were talking to themselves. Instead of concentrating on the ball and following it into their hands, they were thinking about the outcome of the tryouts. Their thoughts were negative: "Don't drop it," "You have to look good," "What's the matter with you?" The thoughts reinforced trying harder which meant tightening up, clenching their jaws, and trying to muscle a response rather than finesse it. Because these athletes were so gifted and because catching the ball was so automatic, they had plenty of time to worry and get distracted while running their pass routes. This worry was destroying them.

Dr. Ogilvie watched the players for a few minutes and then walked over and asked if he could help. He told them that he was impressed with their athletic skills and physical talent, but that he could see they were getting frustrated at not performing the way both he and they knew they could. He spoke with them for a few minutes to get acquainted and then said that he had something he would like them to try. "I know you can perform better than you are doing now. I think my idea will help. Won't you give it a chance?"

Finally, one of the players said "Okay, Doc, I don't have anything to lose; what is it?"

Dr. Ogilvie responded, "I know this is going to sound silly, but please stay with me." He looked at the athletes and said: "What do you say to your woman when you want to make love to her?" The athletes stared at him like he had just been released from a mental hospital; but Ogilvie was insistent. "I know it sounds funny, but it is important! What do you say to your woman when you want her?"

After some embarrassment and kidding, one of the athletes blurted out something like "Hey, Momma, come to your lover man." With that the other athletes started kidding back and forth, becoming relaxed as they joked with each other. "Yea, well, I say 'Momma, I'm going to make you feel like you're in heaven'." Dr. Ogilvie let the athletes joke and tease each other for a couple of minutes, then he interrupted, "That's great! Now, I want you to do something else for me. The next time you go out for a pass, I want you to talk to the ball. I want you to say the things to the ball that you would say to your woman."

The athletes returned to practice and tried the suggestion. Much to their amazement, it worked! They started catching passes and the whole complexion of the tryout changed for them: They became more confident and more relaxed.

Dr. Ogilvie's intervention had accomplished several things. First, the joking about talking to their women on the sidelines had helped the athletes get their minds off their failure and had helped them relax. Next, by asking the athletes to talk to the ball, Dr. Ogilvie had occupied their thoughts during the running of the pass route. If they were talking to the ball, they could not be thinking negative thoughts, the kind that cause them to tighten up.

This change in what you attend to is the same process tennis instructors employ when they ask their students to say "bounce, hit" as the ball bounces and they swing. Not only is attention directed away from the types of thoughts which lead to problems, but in the case of the receivers, it was directed toward thoughts that would cause the athletes to naturally relax their hands. Making love to their woman was an activity totally unrelated to catching a pass. What was not unrelated, however, was the tenderness with which they would have to catch the ball. Just as the athletes' bodies automatically tense when thinking negatively, so would they respond with gentleness to images of tenderness.

FINDING THE RIGHT BUTTONS TO PUSH

Psychologists talk about *conditioned* and *unconditioned* stimuli. An unconditioned stimulus is a happening or object to which we react automatically with a strong physical or emotional response. Thus, a loud unexpected noise automatically elicits a reaction from us. We orient or direct our attention toward the noise. In addition, muscles tighten and there is a startle response.

We tend to see a reaction of fear or anger to a threat, as an unconditioned or automatic response. If we pair what is called a conditioned stimulus, something that normally does not elicit a frightened or angry response, with an unconditioned stimulus, the conditioned stimulus begins to have the same effect on us as the unconditioned one. For example, for years a batter may feel relatively relaxed in the batter's box. Then, he gets hit by a pitched ball. Seeing the ball come at him serves as an unconditioned stimulus. His reaction in trying to get out of the way is automatic. In this instance, he is unsuccessful and is badly injured. A couple of weeks later he has recovered and is back in the batter's box. At this point, even before the pitch is thrown, the batter may begin to react in fear. The relaxation he felt before is gone. It doesn't matter that the pitcher hasn't started his windup, or that the ball isn't coming at him. Mentally, several neutral cues have been associated with getting hit by the ball. Thus, these neutral cues such as standing in the batter's box or facing a left-handed pitcher if the batter was previously hit by a left-hander have now become conditioned stimuli. This means the batter reacts with fear, tension, anxiety, and a startle response, causing him to tighten up and back away from pitches even when they are not threatening. Under these conditions his ability to hit will be interfered with dramatically.

The same type of involuntary reaction occurs in other sports. The diver who finds him or herself unable to keep a reverse-dive close to the board often reacts in a conditioned way to a previous injury or close call. At the start, the diver is not feeling any particular anxiety. Then, as he or she reaches that point in the dive, for example, the hurdle step, where things started to go wrong in the past, a sudden automatic response occurs. Without knowing why, the athlete suddenly finds his or her body thrusting itself out and away from the board. In spite of the absence of any real danger, at an unconscious level, a survival response has taken over. It takes clinical intervention to help an athlete make it past one of these unconscious types of blocks.

Fortunately, just as there are negative conditioned and unconditioned stimuli, there are also positive stimuli. The image of making love to their women was a positive image for the wide receivers. This image led to an automatic response that acted to facilitate performance. Notice that I keep talking about images as conditioned and/or unconditioned stimuli. This is an important point.

FEELING AND EMOTION
VERSUS LOGIC AND REASON

In chapter 11, I presented a logical and rational strategy you can use to help yourself automate performance and speed learning. There is more, however, to athletic performance than logic and reason. Emotions play a major role because they cause us to try harder, to continue when others would stop, to endure pain, to extend ourselves beyond what is expected, or conversely, to quit. These emotions are not controlled through logic and reason but are part of another system and often completely irrational. In fact, the more we try to logically and rationally talk ourselves into feeling a certain way, the less emotion we feel.

Good method actors have discovered situations and experiences, for example, images and sounds that elicit certain feelings. Thus, when actors are in roles requiring that they cry, they often develop tears by mentally recreating for themselves the images associated with past experiences.

Raising emotions can be beneficial if they do not lead to negative thoughts, and if they do not keep you from attending to the right things. The coaches who are able to effectively use a halftime speech to get athletes "out of their heads" and into "winning one for the Gipper" are artists. They paint images to which athletes relate. Your goal is to discover your own images. What makes your hands soft? What causes you to try harder when you are hurting? What gets you to stop feeling sorry for yourself and instead makes you more competitive, more aware of your opponent?

Sometimes, the images are straightforward and rather simple. Dr. Rudi Webster, a practitioner of sport psychology in Australia, tells about changing the images of a group of Australian Rules football players. The problem was that some players were getting tired late in the game and were no longer trying as hard as they could.

In talking with the athletes, Dr. Webster realized the fatigue they were feeling was literally like a "red light," telling them to stop; at least, this was the interpretation they were making. To counter this tendency, Dr. Webster asked them to change the image. He asked the athletes to employ a "thought-stopping" technique. They were to become sensitive to their fatigue and their tendency to let down. When this occurred, they were to center and then to redirect attention to a different image that signaled "go." He asked the athletes to think of a green light and to use that signal to extend themselves. What he did was substitute images by using the centering process to clear out the old image and direct attention to the new one.

To make effective use of a thought-stopping technique, you must find images to which you can redirect attention. In the previous chapter, the emphasis was on redirecting attention to technical or tactical cues. That was because you were trying to alter some physical aspect of performance in addition to speed learning. Once learning is automatic, what you need to alter most often is your attitude or belief, not the physical skill itself. Instead, you need to change those thoughts and feelings that interfere with motivation and normal execution.

A great number of people have seen the movie *Rocky*. As a result, they have paired the theme song from *Rocky* with an image of conquest. This image can be very powerful. For example, when I was running a 10-kilometer race, the organizers had set up giant speakers about 300 yards from the top of a rather steep, 1-mile hill. They were playing the theme from *Rocky*, and the effect on the runners was electric. Fatigued runners were perking up and picking up speed over that last part of the hill. They were smiling and confident, their entire attitude changed by the music.

Other images can also be very powerful for athletes. Examine these examples to find out what motivates you and what gets you to try harder, to feel stronger, and more confident. How about the music from *Chariots of Fire* or *Flash Dance*? Stories and images associated with individuals who beat the odds or make real sacrifices are inspiring to most of us. *Brian's Song*, the television production of a terminally ill football player's relationship with a teammate, a child battling a terminal illness, a mother protecting her child—all create images you can use to motivate yourself. Many athletes react to animal stories which are associated with loyalty and sacrifice. We react to animal images and can often feel ourselves soar with eagles or run with stallions.

You need to arm yourself with images you can recall when you find yourself in doubt. Sometimes those images are supportive; sometimes they are threatening. Maryanne Dickerson's image was of her father as she came into the stadium at the world championships in Helsinki, Finland. She was a few hundred yards from the finish of the marathon and about a hundred yards behind a Russian runner. All she could think about was what her father said as she left: "Don't you let any of those Russians beat you." The reaction to her father's command was an emotional button for her, releasing the energy she needed at a critical point.

Ali, the boxer, had his own set of images. He would talk about "floating like a butterfly, stinging like a bee." That image and that self-talk would help keep him on his toes, dancing and jabbing. Even in the face of punishment, he could fall back on that image and those words to get himself moving. Tom Petranoff uses the words "this is it," and the music from the popular song with the same title to pump himself up and to help him focus his concentration on the javelin.

To encourage you to develop an idea of the images you use, watch some video tapes of your own play. Get someone to record your performance. Take the material and edit it down until you have a series of performances of the kind in which you want to systematically engage. Then, try and emotionally describe the feelings that you actually had as you were playing in each of those segments. Do this in two ways: First, simply observe your own performance in an objective, unemotional way as you watch the tape. While doing this, try and think of images of animals that might describe your own play, for example, like a panther—smooth, strong, and unyielding. Usually this will allow you to find an image such as a running horse, which is associated with many automatic feelings. Thus, when you create the feelings without having to try, your image becomes a stimulus that leads to the desired response.

Next, place yourself in the situation once more and review the film once again. Placing yourself in the picture as you are watching it this time, relive it to see if you can recover the same emotional intensity that you felt then. This is a process that I ask entire teams to go through at film sessions. For example, if I show a group of basketball players a video where the team was performing well, I will not ask them to focus on techniques or tactics. Those are automatic responses for skilled players. Instead, I will sensitize them to the differences in their emotions, to the intensity of their feelings. I will get them to describe that intensity, to observe that "they were not inside their heads." As they watch, they can feel the intensity and see that their concentration was totally focused on the game and on what was going on around them. They were free from internal distractions.

As you see that intensity in your own performance, try and

develop feelings and images associated with the intensity. For example, you may have felt your hair flying back as you moved or you had a sense of floating effortlessly. Having identified some images and feelings, you have cues and things to attend to the next time you get into the activity. You can learn to use these images to elevate your level of play, to motivate yourself, to get out of your head and into the game, to forget about mechanics and just let your performance flow.

MIXING EMOTIONS AND REASON

The way to combine emotions and reason in order to have the best of both worlds is to use your logic and analytical abilities to identify not only ways to push your own emotional buttons, but to anticipate the situations where that type of button pushing is desirable. Then, you systematically and analytically rehearse remembering to push those buttons. Let me give you an example of the process.

Begin by contrasting past successful situations with unsuccessful ones as you did in chapter 8. This time, ask yourself what your feelings were and what seemed to trigger these feelings. What was it about the competitive situation that pushed the emotional button?

Next, take the negative situation and mentally rehearse it. As you do, you want to make a conscious attempt to become very aware of those cues that create negative feelings and/or tension. The reason you want to attend to these is because you want to become aware of rising tension early enough to modify it before the tension is so high that you cannot control it. Thus, a tennis player may find herself thinking, "I hope she doesn't hit it to my backhand." That thought would signal her that muscle tension is increasing. Thus, before a mistake is actually made and before tension accelerates to the point of being out of control, the athlete has an opportunity to make a correction.

Your objective is to become aware of self-defeating thoughts associated with your performance errors, thoughts such as "Blew it again, stupid. Can't you do anything right?" You also want to become aware of the associated feelings of tension in certain muscles, such as in the neck and the shoulders.

As you become aware of these thoughts and feelings by mentally rehearsing the sequence, use them as cues to center in order to clear out distractions and to adjust muscle tension levels. Thus, the negative feelings, instead of leading to more negative feelings, cue you to respond in a more constructive way.

The difference now is that after completing the centering, you redirect attention to the emotional images and cues as opposed to tactical or technical cues. In the previous tennis example, the player countered by relaxing and by thinking of herself as a panther ready to spring. The images and thoughts you identify should change your attitude. As you can see from the example, these images have no direct relationship to tactical or technical aspects of performance. The last thing you want to do with a highly skilled performance during a competition is think too much about it. Instead, you automatically act to alter your feelings and tension so the movements simply happen once again. Your images put you in the right frame of mind to allow your body to perform effectively and automatically. Ali would redirect his attention to "float like a butterfly, sting like a bee," and that would automatically cause him to jab. An opponent's punch and the pain associated with it would signal him to center and to "float like a butterfly, sting like a bee."

In a similar way, a runner's pain might serve as the signal to center and to get into the image of a running stag. For Maryanne Dickerson it was an image of her father commanding her not to let the Russians beat her.

FOCUS ON FEELINGS AND IMAGES, NOT ON OUTCOME

Until you get your attitude turned around, it will be important for you to remember to focus on images that create the desired feelings. Turning around your attitude simply means changing negative thoughts in problem situations. I am not implying that you need to change some basic personality characteristic that affects your whole life. Instead, an attitude is simply a set of feelings associated with a particular sport situation. In this sense we all have a "bad attitude" at one time or another.

Getting back to desired images, you are better off if you stay away from images associated with the immediate outcome of your performance, especially if you lack self-confidence in the performance situation. Instead, think about the process of performing, of trying or striving as opposed to winning. If you are striving or trying, you are going to be getting positive feedback because you can be successful independent of the outcome: "It's not whether you win, but how you play the game that counts.

DO NOT OVERUSE
YOUR EMOTIONAL RESOURCES

You do have a limited amount of emotional energy. To expect yourself to be "up" and intense all the time is unrealistic. It is an impossible goal. If you expect that much of yourself, you will quickly be disappointed and you will likely burn out.

A diver told me that he had great workouts on Monday and Tuesday, but that Wednesday, Thursday, and Friday were much more difficult. On these days he seemed emotionally down and fatigued, and he was giving in to these feelings, reaching the point where he expected to feel badly on those days. When he felt down, the diver felt helpless and gave up quite easily. He wanted me to help him have the same energy and enthusiasm on those days as he did on Monday and Tuesday.

After talking about it, he was able to realize that going through a difficult list of dives day after day did take its toll. Emotionally and physically, he was going to have some down times. A much more realistic goal than believing he could be up all the time was learning to "be up" for a series of 10 dives, the number of dives he would have to do in competition. Although I could not promise to have him emotionally up all of the time, I helped him develop a program for picking himself up for those 10 dives. In this way, he would develop confidence in his ability to turn it on when he needed to.

The diver searched for his own emotional buttons, and he worked out a rehearsal program as well as a program that he implemented in practice. The important point was that he did not try to use the program on each dive. Instead, he limited the application to once a week. His goal was to begin by picking himself up for a couple of dives during one practice where he felt down. Then, after he had success with just two dives, he was to extend his goal to encompass three dives and so on. Eventually, he would be able to get himself ready for all 10 dives. Remember, do not burn yourself out needlessly. Learn to turn it on when it counts.

SUMMARY

Chapter 12 demonstrates techniques which reduce distractions and negative thoughts during competition. It will be important for you to keep several points in mind:

1. Tension can automatically increase in response to negative thoughts. Conversely, we can identify *positive* thoughts that allow us to automatically relax and to concentrate more effectively.

2. To change your feelings, you need to find the right buttons to push. These buttons are images and sensations that are associated with positive emotional feelings. Intellectual arguments or insight into "why you feel the way you do" will not result in the desired changes.

3. When you lack confidence in an athletic situation, you are more likely to control your feelings by directing attention to images associated with *trying*, as opposed to images linked with *winning*.

4. Set realistic goals for yourself. Do not expect to be emotionally intense 100% of the time. Learn to turn it on when it really counts.

Chapter 13 will outline additional techniques which simulate actual situations in competition in order to familiarize athletes with unusual conditions and surroundings.

13

Mental Rehearsal to Simulate Competition

One of the reasons that competitive efforts in championship games, such as the World Series and the Olympics, are sometimes below what we expected is that the competitive events prior to the finals were different. Often, rules change in championships to accommodate sponsors, television networks, and fans. In events like the world championships in track and field, or the Olympic games, the number of competitors is dramatically increased and the logistical problems that this creates, can play havoc with the athletes' ability to concentrate and to keep their minds on performance.

The problems posed by new conditions can be dramatically multiplied if athletes enter these situations with self-doubts. Self-doubts cause you to look for problems. When you lack confidence, what might be a minor irritation under more normal conditions can easily get magnified into a major problem. Even those athletes who can put up with the press during the regular season can suddenly become irritated by the camera that gets stuck in their faces around championship time. When food is not exactly to an athlete's liking, when people are not as friendly as expected, when an official makes a poor call, some athletes are unable to cope in highly competitive situations. Even after the problem has been corrected, for example, the line call is reversed, an athlete is so upset that the problem continues to distract him or her. The distractions can become excuses for poor performance and for fear. Even if the distractions do not become excuses, they often serve to make you more sensitive to problems, to look harder for the next mistake by a linesman or an official.

Athletes who perform better often find their own ways of releasing the pressure. Mel Rosen, our Olympic sprint coach for 1984, tells a story about the 1976 Olympics. At the Olympic games, all of the competitors are isolated from coaches and noncompetitors for a period prior to the start of their event. At this time, they sit quietly in a holding area or waiting room. For many, this is a very stressful time. Without something to do, something to keep their minds occupied, they have too much time to think and worry. Thus, they often feel some immediate relief when they are finally told to move out onto the track for the start of the race. Once again, they have structure and something to do.

On this particular occasion in 1976, the sprinters were led onto the field, and according to coach Rosen, one of the favorites was feeling confident and ready. All of the athletes lined up at the blocks and as they were about to settle into the blocks for the start of the race, an official stopped them. An awards ceremony was about to take place, so they could not start the race at that time, a condition the athletes had not experienced in other meets. All of the sprinters were led back to a holding area to wait. With this unexpected delay, the tension grew unbelievably.

All of a sudden, Hasley Crawford, the ultimate winner of the race, started screaming at the top of his lungs. Everyone else just tightened up; they did not know what to do. When they were led back on the track, Crawford was the only one that had released the excess tension, and he left them all in the blocks. That is one way to relieve tension!

The world championships in track and field in Helsinki in 1983 was a real eye-opener for many American athletes. They learned that for these championships, and for the Olympic games, the competitive environment would be unlike the meet conditions they were used to. Throughout the year, track athletes travel to meets on their own. They need not live with other athletes. Their competition is not stretched out over a 10-day period. Thus, they arrive, compete, and leave. In Helsinki, and in the Olympics, they check into the village and then may have 10 days before they race. Or, they may find that they have several races spread out over several days.

The timing of the preliminaries, semifinals, and finals is to suit the spectators and television, not the athletes' training.

The food in the village, no matter how good, is mass prepared. Sleep is a problem, because when one athlete wants to sleep, another wants to celebrate. Just when one wants to be left alone to concentrate, another wants to socialize to reduce his or her anxiety. Because of the number of competitors, athletes find themselves unable to tell how well others are performing, or to estimate how well they will have to run in their heat to advance. Throwers and jumpers who are used to having six attempts in a row find themselves engaged in two, three-throw competitions. They have three throws in a preliminary to qualify for the final. Then, if they make the final, they get another three throws. Psychologically, only having three throws increases the pressure that athletes feel.

If their own internal concerns are not enough, external distractions such as the press, loudspeaker announcements, awards ceremonies, all add to the pressure. Furthermore, they may be concerned about the political nature of the games. If they need excuses because they lack confidence, they can worry about terrorists, traffic jams, or any of a hundred other very real concerns. It is not difficult at all for athletes with even minor self-doubts to find excuses for not performing up to their level. Too often, the groundwork for failure is laid and the race is lost before the competition ever begins. Because this can happen to anyone, it is important to reduce as many of these potential distractions as possible. It also is important to teach athletes to recover quickly from distractions. Even if you cannot prevent the unexpected, you can learn to quickly recover!

One of the ways you can reduce distractions is to simulate as many of the actual competitive conditions as you can. Much of this simulation must be mental because the opportunity to actually practice under Olympic or Super Bowl or Stanley Cup conditions simply does not exist.

Whenever possible, you should supplement your mental rehearsal of competitive conditions with external visual and auditory aids. I often encourage athletes to put pictures of the competitive conditions up around their homes and at practice areas. I encourage them to concentrate on those pictures, to imagine walking into those conditions. You can do this by asking yourself what it is going to feel like, what you will see as you move out onto the field. By going over these things in advance and by becoming used to them, they will lose some of their uniqueness and along with that, some of their ability to serve as distractors.

If you know in advance that certain conditions will exist, and that those conditions will be distracting, then practice controlling those distractions through mental imagery, and through actually creating those conditions during practices. Use thought-stopping to stop negative thinking, then center, and redirect your attention to the competition following the procedures outlined in chapter 12.

In the United States, we are at a disadvantage relative to some of the Eastern block countries in many international competitions. This is especially true in events like the Olympic games. Under our system, the coaches for the Olympic games often have little actual control over the athlete. In many cases they do not even know them. Whereas coaches and officials from the Soviet Union, East Germany, China, Cuba, Romania, Yugoslavia, and Czechoslovakia have much greater control over their athletes and can protect them from many of the distractions created by the press and by officials.

A system like the one used in the United States places the great responsibility of functioning independently on the athlete. Obviously, there are some advantages to this. It does mean, however, that you need to work a little harder to prepare yourself to handle some of the distractions that others do not have to worry about.

You need to build confidence in your ability to recover from the negative effects of frustration. You need to train yourself not to make excuses, and to use your own negative thoughts as cues to adjust tension and to clear out distractions. You must be able to redirect your concentration to more positive cues, to your music, to your emotional images, or to the mechanics of your performance. The only way to accomplish this goal is with self-discipline and practice. If you want to be the best, you must do your homework, both on and off the field, both mental and physical.

SUMMARY

Chapter 13 explores the reasons why competitive efforts in international or elite class sport events frequently are below expectations:

1. The competitive events prior to the finals are different.
2. Housing, food, interaction with other athletes and with the press are unfamiliar and therefore stressful.
3. Because of extreme distractions, athletes with self-doubts find easy excuses for not performing up to their level.

As it is impossible to actually practice under Olympic or Super Bowl conditions, athletes are advised to *mentally* simulate the competitive conditions, augmented by external visual and auditory aids.

Chapter 14 will point out some pitfalls that can make athletes their own worst enemy.

14

Integration of Mind and Body

From my experience, the techniques outlined in this book can be very effective. With some self-discipline and dedication, most athletes can use these techniques to speed learning, to gain control over their level of muscle tension and concentration, and to improve the skill and consistency of performance. Still, we are all different and nothing is perfect. For this reason, I would like to introduce a few cautions, sensitizing you to some things which make it easier for you to use this material.

DON'T BE YOUR OWN WORST ENEMY

The same competitiveness and need to excel and to be in control that drives many athletes to greatness also drives many athletes to self-destruction. Managing the fine line between talent and temperament is often extremely difficult. The worst thing you can do for yourself is to expect too much. The demand for personal perfection and control can haunt the talented athlete.

1. When you cannot accept your own vulnerability and imperfection, you cannot accept mistakes. This means that the world must be as you want it to be. When it is not, frustration builds and you feed on distractions. You use minor irritations as excuses. It is easier to blame others,

or the competitive conditions, or a minor injury than it is to accept your own limitations.

2. Feelings that you must control your own destiny and life can become so strong you cannot accept help from others. To even think you might need assistance is to admit the weakness that you are trying so desperately to conquer. "If I can't control it, no one can." You can see this tendency in yourself when you flare up and get enraged at constructive criticism or suggestions designed to help you regain control over a competitive situation.

3. The need to be perfect can keep you from being able to prioritize activities and from accepting the fact that some aspects of your life will not be as you would like them to be. The athlete who wants to be the best, while earning straight A's in school and maintaining a meaningful social life, is often expecting too much.

LEARN TO SET REASONABLE GOALS FOR YOURSELF

Many athletes set extremely unreasonable goals for themselves. Perhaps the biggest roadblock to gaining better mental control is the expectancy that training procedures will somehow free you from anxiety and self-doubts forever. These athletes do not ever want to make a "mental error," to "choke," or to "feel anxious."

You need to think about mental skills as you would about physical skills. You need to plan a program for making gradual corrections. For example, instead of feeling that you should never let anxiety get the better of you, you need to see first how frequently the problem occurs.

As you make plans for gaining control over tension and concentration, describe your problems in terms of the frequency of occurrence and the intensity of the problem: How strong are the feelings? How tight the muscles? How long does it take you to recover from the disturbance?

Next, sit down with a coach and establish some reasonable expectations for change. What should you be trying to modify? You can never prepare for everything. The unexpected will happen and you will react. Your goal should not be to *prevent* the unexpected, your goal should be to *reduce* the frequency of the unexpected through better planning and anticipation, and to *speed recovery* from the unexpected. You should learn to use the centering and attention redirection procedures to prevent mistakes from piling on top of each other.

DO NOT BECOME OVERCONFIDENT

Have you ever asked yourself why it is that you seem to repeat the same mistakes? Tom Petranoff is a good example of someone with this type of problem. Prior to his world record throw, he realized that he needed to control his tendency to become distracted and too tense. He practiced procedures designed to control muscle tension in his throwing arm and he learned to concentrate, to shut out the normal distractors. The results were nothing less than sensational: He broke the world record in the javelin by more than 10 feet!

What happened immediately after that throw? Many new distractions entered Tom's life. Suddenly, he was big news and he was being called and interviewed constantly. He had to renegotiate contracts with shoe companies. Enjoying the attention, he allowed it to interfere with his normal training. His success generated additional pressure. "Maybe my throw was just lucky?" He had to throw another incredible effort to demonstrate it was not an accident. This pressure increased muscle tension again, something he thought he had solved. The only difference was that now it was a new set of thoughts and worries that were triggering the muscle tension. He had to become sensitive to these.

As if the pressures mentioned were not bad enough, announcers would disturb Tom's concentration during the middle of a throw. Because he was now a world record thrower, everyone wanted to know when he was throwing. He would be in his run-up and hear the loud speaker blare: "Tom Petranoff, world record holder in the javelin, is now throwing." He conquered these new problems, but not without some backsliding first. There is always more to work on!

"KNOW WHEN TO HOLD THEM,
KNOW WHEN TO FOLD THEM"

You've got to know when to hold them,
Know when to fold them.
Know when to walk away,
Know when to run.

Kenny Rogers, "The Gambler"

As in Kenny Rogers's song "The Gambler" none of us has a winning hand all the time. Mental discipline and attention control training means learning to play to your strengths and to recognize, correct, and minimize your weaknesses. It means knowing "when to hold them."

Within limits, you can be what you want to be. No one has ever realized his or her full potential. There has never been an analysis of a world record or of any team's performance that did not identify ways upon which the performance could have been improved. Sometimes the key to expanding your own potential is to ease off.

INTEGRATION OF MIND AND BODY

As you can see from the contents of this book, sport is the one situation in life that truly provides the opportunity for the pursuit of excellence through the total integration of mind and body. A business executive may perform quite well without a magnificent body. To achieve his or her full potential, however, the athlete must develop both. We are on the threshold of accomplishing that dream. It is within our grasp.

SUMMARY

Chapter 14 contends that with proper self-discipline and dedication, the techniques outlined in this book can be very effective. Sport provides the opportunity for the pursuit of excellence through the total integration of mind and body. Because athletes are individuals with different personalities, the following cautions will prevent competitors from being their own worst enemy:

1. Competitiveness and a need to excel may lead to a demand for personal perfection and control which could drive a talented athlete to self-destruction.

2. A desire for total control can give some athletes the mistaken idea that it is a weakness to accept help and advice from others.

3. The need to be perfect can prevent athletes from prioritizing certain aspects of their life and goad them into setting unrealistic goals for themselves.

Chapter 15 will outline a training program for mental rehearsal both on and off the field.

15

A Training Model
You Can Follow

In the next few pages an outline for a training model you can follow as you develop your own mental skills is provided. Although I will place some time limit on each aspect of the program, you should remember that these are somewhat arbitrary. There are tremendous individual differences that should be considered. For example, you may find that your skills in a particular area are already highly developed, that you do not need to take a week or two to develop them. On the other hand, some athletes require a great deal more time than indicated.

In addition, you should remember that the skills you develop build upon each other. This means that you continue to use them and practice them, even after the initial training. Just as you continue to maintain basic skills and a basic level of physical fitness in your sport, so, too, you need to maintain your mental skills, practicing them on a daily basis.

One additional caution before outlining the program: Do not make the mistake of moving too quickly. Sometimes athletes rush because they are eager to learn. At other times we rush because things seem so simple; we are sure we have the answer. It has been my experience that most athletes do not have the answer as quickly as they would like to believe. Things are not always as they seem. Going a bit slowly now will pay off later!

WEEK 1: FINDING YOUR OPTIMAL LEVEL OF AROUSAL

The material in chapters 4, 5, and 7 will be helpful in getting you to become much more sensitive to your own optimal level of arousal. I have provided you here with a general strategy of self-observation:

1. You want to monitor tension levels and that "racing" feeling associated with a pounding heart under different levels of pressure. Observe yourself in both practice and actual competitive situations. If you do not have the opportunity to compete, at least make an effort to manipulate the pressure you feel in practice. You can do this by increasing the importance of your performance in the practice situation (e.g., challenging yourself to set a personal record, betting with others on the outcome, performing in front of a critical audience).

2. Identify performance-relevant muscle groups. What muscles affect your performance? What muscles provide an early indication that you are starting to tighten up? Use the form below to record your level of tension in various muscle groups under both practice and competitive conditions. Make sure that you check tension in the following major groups: (a) face, neck, and jaw; (b) shoulders, chest, and arms; (c) calves and thighs.

3. Not only do you want to determine how you feel in relevant muscle groups under both practice and competitive conditions, but you want to check tension in different situations or when performing different skills. To do this, you will have to identify those times during your sport when you have enough time to check tension levels briefly. Appendix A will help you identify some of these times in your particular sport. In general, you want to see if the following factors affect your level of tension: (a) person factors; does it make a difference who you are competing against? (b) skill factors; are you more or less tense when executing particular skills (e.g., throwing vs. hitting, reverse-dives vs. front-dives); (c) situation factors; do particular situations make a difference in terms

of the tension you feel? For example, are you more tense at the start, in the middle, or at the end of a performance? Do particular competitive arenas or surfaces create tension?

Although I have only listed three general areas to cover, I am asking you for a great deal of information. Do not rush through this section too quickly. Remember, you cannot cor-

TABLE 15.1

Muscle Tension Levels

PRACTICE	1	2	3	4	5	6	7	8	9	10
	TOTAL RELAXATION				AVERAGE TENSION					VERY TENSE
Face, neck, jaw	—	—	—	—	—	—	—	—	—	—
Shoulders, chest, arms	—	—	—	—	—	—	—	—	—	—
Calves & thighs	—	—	—	—	—	—	—	—	—	—

*Note: Use the above chart as an example, and fill one out for each of the competitive conditions (e.g., person, skill, situation factors) likely to affect your tension.

TABLE 15.2

Muscle Tension Levels

COMPETITION	1	2	3	4	5	6	7	8	9	10
	TOTAL RELAXATION				AVERAGE TENSION					VERY TENSE
Face, neck, jaw	—	—	—	—	—	—	—	—	—	—
Shoulders, chest, arms	—	—	—	—	—	—	—	—	—	—
Calves & thighs	—	—	—	—	—	—	—	—	—	—

rect inappropriate levels of tension if you are not aware of them. Becoming sensitive to your own body is the first step in gaining greater self-control.

Keep a diary so that you can record your feelings and keep track of those particular individuals, skills, or game situations that affect your level of tension and your ability to perform.

WEEK 2: IDENTIFYING SOURCES OF DISTRACTION

Just as you take the time to monitor your feelings of tension under different competitive conditions when performing different skills, and in different situations, so, too, do you want to keep track of your thoughts. In particular, you want to be sensitive to those thoughts that indicate a lack of confidence, or a negative attitude. Remember, we all have negative attitudes at certain times, and we all lack confidence at times. The important thing for you to do is to identify when those times occur, and to identify the thoughts and feelings associated with them.

Once again, it will be important for you to keep a daily diary so that you can record and remember what is going on. The diary does not need to be complicated, but you need to do the following: (a) describe the situation you are in when confidence lags or frustration develops; (b) identify the particular event (e.g., a missed shot at a critical time) or image (e.g., seeing a more skilled or physically fit competitor) that served to trigger the negative thinking; (c) write down the thought and feeling content: "I saw this slim bouncy person on the other side of the net and felt fat. I started thinking I couldn't compete and didn't belong on the same court."

Let me sensitize you to some critical times, when most athletes have lapses in their ability to continue to think positively. At the following times you will want to monitor your own thoughts and feelings: (a) a few days before the competition (particularly true if the competition is a major one, and if you are "tapering training" in order to prepare); (b) immediately prior to the beginning of a contest (while warming up); (c) in between events, tricks, plays, shots, and so on;

(d) at critical times in the competition (the last minute of a close game, or a must shot, for example).

As you identify your thoughts and the images or triggers that cause them, you also want to become aware of associated feelings—that is, muscle tension. Thus, you are combining the skills and information gained in both weeks 1 and 2. When you complete your entries in your diary, you will want to be able to describe how thoughts affect muscle tension.

WEEK 3: IDENTIFYING POSITIVE IMAGES

In week 3, I want you to find out what makes you feel good about yourself. What motivates you? What makes you try harder and refuse to give up? What images, sounds, thoughts can you use to "turn yourself around"?

First, identify *general* characteristics or successes that help you feel good about yourself. For example, the knowledge that you arc a hard worker and willing to sacrifice can help you feel positive. Second, to feel confident, you will have to remember the *particular* situation you are concerned about.

The fact that you were a high school star in a particular sport will not necessarily convince you that you can star in college. If you have doubts in a particular situation, you need to find as many things that are directly related to that situation as you can. If you cannot find support for believing that you can control the outcome and win, find thoughts and images that at least make you feel confident in your ability to perform, win or lose. Here are some things you can do:

1. Interview a coach or friend. Try and get someone else to help remind you of your strengths relative to other athletes'. If you are like most athletes, you have a tendency to be too critical of yourself, and support from others can be helpful.

2. Pick a couple of past situations to compare. One where you felt confident should be contrasted with one where you did not. What was the difference in the things you said to yourself? What was the difference in your tension level? What was the difference in terms of how you responded to unexpected events or to your own mistakes?

3. Set aside some time to listen to different kinds of music. Identify music that "sends a chill down your spine" or picks you up. Do the same thing with pictures. Go through some sport pictures and pictures of animals. Try and find some pictures that are inspirational to you. If you can get pictures of yourself that remind you of your own toughness and ability that is even better. Surround yourself with reminders of your successes, with evidence of the type of attitude and feelings you want to maintain when the going gets tough.

4. Who are your heroes? Who are the inspirational people in your life? Who are the people you would least like to let down? What is it about these people that motivates and challenges you? Are you afraid of rejection, afraid to disappoint them? Can you feel their support? It does not matter whether you are motivated by fear (afraid to let someone down) or motivated by love (a desire to please by doing something for someone else). The important thing is to clarify in your own mind what it is in others that serves to get you to do your best. Take the time to write down who can motivate you, and how they can do it. What do they need to say and/or do? Mentally prepare yourself to call on these images when you feel a lack of confidence.

WEEK 4: LEARN TO CENTER

The actual process of centering does not take very long. It is very important, however, that you consciously discipline yourself to engage in the centering procedure at critical times. Use the two appendixes to help identify *when* you should center in your particular sport, and to *what* you should pay attention after centering.

Once again, keep a diary to record your progress and to ensure the fact that you are actually building the centering into your normal routine. Review the material in chapters 9 and 10. I want you to become completely involved in the centering process for at least a week. You should center at the following times:

1. Just prior to the start of an activity in order to develop a consistent level of tension;
2. Immediately prior to the initiation of a new activity (e.g., at the end of a tumbling run in gymnastics; between points in tennis);
3. Just prior to making a critical decision during a time-out or in the last few seconds of a game.

Practice your centering both on and off the field. Using the tension scale presented earlier, see how much you can alter your own level of tension while sitting, walking down the street, performing. For example, estimate the level of tension in your neck, shoulders, and chest right now and assign a number to it. Now, inhale deeply and as you do, raise your tension level. How high does it go? Next, relax the muscles in neck and shoulders as you exhale. Now, how low does the tension rating go?

Repeat this exercise throughout the day under different conditions. Keep a record of each day's activity and see how much control you are getting over time. Challenge yourself to be able to keep someone from lifting you. Again, test the development of this skill on a daily basis.

WEEK 5: CHANGE A NEGATIVE ATTITUDE

By the time you get to week 5, you should be sensitive to various problem areas. What I want you to do is pick a particular situation where you lack confidence, or where you lose control over anger and frustration. Pick only one situation. Chapter 12 will help you with this exercise.

Identify a particular time, opponent, or skill that is causing you problems. Keep track of your performance and feelings in that situation. Be able to tell how frequently the problem occurs (e.g., 10 times a game, once a month) and to measure the intensity of your feelings. Use a 10-point scale with 1 being not feeling it at all, 5 being average, and 10 being extremely intense. Finally, be able to tell how long the feelings last once they develop. In other words, how long does it take for you to forget about it and get back into the game?

You need to pick a problem that occurs frequently enough (at least once a game) so you can see if change is occurring. In addition, set yourself some reasonable goals and measure the change. By knowing how long the interference usually lasts, we can tell if your attempt to "put it out of your mind" is working. If a tennis player allows a bad call to affect her for 3 points, and after training only allows it to affect her for 2 points, it means progress.

Your effort for the week should be to see how much control you can get over a negative self-defeating attitude. This might be a negative attitude about practice that keeps you from putting out, or from controlling anger when you do not perform as perfectly as you would like. Do this with the following steps:

1. Take a baseline measure (observe yourself) to see how frequent, intense, and long lasting the problem is.
2. Identify the specific situation within which the problem occurs.
3. Describe any negative changes in tension and in thought content that occur at this time. What feelings and thoughts will tell you it is time to center and redirect attention?
4. Identify what it is that you should be directing your attention to after centering (use Appendixes).
5. Center and redirect your attention to more positive thoughts and images.
6. Keep track of how long it takes you to regain control.

As you work on this exercise, do not be upset if you find yourself having negative thoughts and having to center a large number of times in a very short period. Often, we can put a frustration out of our mind for a few seconds only to find it come back. If that is the case, the advantage you have is that you are getting much practice which will really help you when the chips are down. If you find yourself becoming discouraged, recognize that this, too, provides an opportunity for you to use your own motivational images to turn things around. Keep track and discuss your progress with someone to whom you can relate and trust.

WEEK 6: MENTAL REHEARSAL

Use this week to demonstrate to yourself how you can use mental rehearsal procedures like those outlined in chapters 7, 11, and 13 to improve the consistency of performance. Pick a perfomance segment (e.g., a particular motor sequence like a free throw in basketball, or pitching in baseball) on which you want to work.

1. Define for yourself your current level of performance. How often do errors occur? Where in the performance sequence do you become aware of problems? How consistent is the performance right now? For example, a bowler might be able to tell me that he picks up the 5-10 split three out of five times. He may also be able to identify that when he misses, it is because he hits the 5 pin too hard. A diver might tell me that she gets scores ranging from 4 to 8 on a particular dive, and that they average 6.

2. Identify a place in the performance sequence (typically at the start) when you can center. At the same time, specify to what you need to direct your attention immediately after centering, just as you begin to perform. Because you are trying to improve the consistency of performance, this may be a technical self-instruction, or a correction for the particular problem you have been having. A diver might remind him or herself to bring the arms up closer to the body to reduce a lean, for example.

3. Walk yourself through the performance sequence, calling attention to the feelings you have in your body at the beginning, at each transition point, and as you conclude the behavior.

4. Spend 10 minutes twice a day sitting down and mentally rehearsing the entire sequence. Begin by rehearsing somewhat slower than the activity actually takes, and during the week increase the speed until it is in real time. Concentrate on developing the images and feelings that you would actually perceive as you go through the activity. You literally want to feel your muscles contract.

5. As you engage in the rehearsal process, emphasize a positive attitude and feeling. See yourself being successful, and feel the success.

6. In addition to rehearsing the activity twice each day, take the time to mentally rehearse immediately prior to actually engaging in the performance. Find time to do this on the field or in the competitive situation (e.g., a batter would visualize hitting just before stepping back into the batter's box).

7. Record your level of performance so that you can examine any changes in level of consistency.

The key to your success in the use of any mental training program is consistency—consistency in terms of practice and in terms of keeping good records. A diary is important and will be very valuable to future as well as to immediate efforts.

SUMMARY

Chapter 15 outlines a training model for developing mental skills. It is divided into six weekly steps:

1. Week 1 attempts to find the athlete's optimal level of arousal.
2. Week 2 identifies sources of distractions.
3. Week 3 identifies positive images.
4. Week 4 teaches when to center.
5. Week 5 changes negative attitudes.
6. Week 6 demonstrates the use of mental rehearsal procedures.

Appendix A will present suggestions about when it might be useful to center during a particular competition and will identify some technical or tactical cues to direct attention to after centering.

Appendix B will give detailed attentional requirements for different sports.

Appendix A

When to Center and to What to Direct Attention

Table A.1 presents some suggestions regarding when you might find it useful to center during a particular competition. The table also identifies some of the technical and/or tactical cues that you could direct attention to following centering. This assumes that your level of performance is already highly skilled and that some other aspect of your own performance hasn't been identified as a key. *Before* using the particular focus suggested here, you should check it out with a coach or someone else who knows you and the sport!

TABLE A.1

When to Center and to What to Direct Attention

SPORT OR POSITION	WHEN TO CENTER	WHAT TO ATTEND TO
Aikido	Any time there is sufficient distance between you and opponents to allow 2-second breath.	Single mental instruction (e.g., to shift from point to point to assess).
Archery	Immediately prior to release of the arrow.	Sight picture.
Auto Racing	Immediately prior to the start of the race.	To starting signal.
	Immediately after any major stress (e.g., spin, near crash, momentary loss of control).	To a reassuring self-instruction followed by direction of attention to the task of driving.

TABLE A.1 (cont.)

	In response to any negative thoughts.	Redirect concentration toward the mechanics of driving.
Badminton	Immediately prior to serving and/or to receipt of serve.	Both performers may, following the centering, give themself *one* instruction (e.g., attack, etc.), and then immediately direct concentration externally to the birdie.
	On points where a high allows time for a quick assessment of tension.	Attention is always directed to the birdie.
Baseball	As a hitter, just prior to the pitcher's delivery.	Following the adjustment of muscle tension, concentration is focused on the ball.
	As a pitcher, just after receipt of the catcher's sign and selection of a pitch.	A single self-instruction is typically given (focusing attention on execution), like "low and away," "follow-through," "eye on the catcher's glove." Then, attention is focused on the rocking motion that initiates the wind-up.
	Any player can center in response to negative thoughts but should time the centering so it is complete as the pitcher begins the delivery of the ball.	Turn to a single positive self-instruction and then to the ball.
	As a baserunner, just before an attempted steal, bunt, hit and run.	Adjust tension, then direct concentration to the single cue that is most relevant (e.g., in the case of stealing, it may be reading the pitcher or getting a certain lead-off.
	On certain fielding plays, especially in the infield, it may be useful to center to avoid rushing the throw, particularly if you have just made an error.	Momentary tension adjustment, self-instruction of "relax, eye on the target, throw."

TABLE A.1 (cont.)

Basketball	Immediately prior to any free-throw attempt.	Momentary tension adjustment, especially neck and shoulders, then eye on the target.
	When inbounding the ball and you are under pressure.	Momentary tension adjustment and self-instruction to "relax, find the open man."
	Immediately after committing a foul or losing the ball on a turnover.	Momentary tension adjustment and self-instruction to "easy, back in the game."
	At the end of any time-out, just as the whistle blows to return to the court.	Momentary adjustment of tension, single instruction that gets you to focus on your own immediate task.
Billiards	Immediately prior to stroking the ball. Centering will occur following the mental rehearsal of the shot.	Momentary adjustment of breathing and tension, then direction of attention to the spot on the ball you intend to strike (or to the total sight picture if you don't focus on a single spot).
Boxing	Just as you move to the center of the ring, before the action has started.	Adjust tension in neck and shoulders, single reminder (e.g., "jab") and direct attention to the other boxer.
	Immediately after a knockdown (when you are receiving a count).	Adjust tension, quickly check your need for more time to recover. Direct attention to clinching, moving away or coming back strong depending on your feelings.
	When you have just knocked down your opponent and he is receiving a count.	Quickly adjust tension level and remind yourself of your corner's instructions for this situation.
	When fatigued but while tied up in a clinch.	Relax tension and use breath to speed recovery. Momentary shift to positive self-instruction, "now is the time to pour it on." Redirect attention to execution.

TABLE A.1 (cont.)

Diving	After coming to attention on the board or tower and just before beginning the approach.	Adjust muscle tension in neck and shoulders, feel yourself press down against the board or platform as you exhale. Single reminder (e.g., "press on entry," "high hurdle"), then direct attention to the take-off.
Drag Racing	After moving to the line, and immediately prior to the beginning of the timing-light sequence.	Adjust muscle tension in upper body. Single reminder of technical or tactical aspect of the race. Direction of concentration to the timing lights.
Fencing	Immediately prior to the start of the contest.	Adjustment of muscle tension and breathing. Single tactical or technical instruction. Direction of concentration on the most task-relevant external cue (e.g., opponent's position or foil).
	At any point during the competition when there is a momentary break in the action.	Same as above.
Figure Skating	Immediately prior to the beginning of a school figure.	Adjust neck and shoulder muscle tension, feel skates press against the ice on the exhale. Concentrate on figure and flow.
	Immediately prior to the beginning of a program.	Adjust tension level. Single tactical or technical or attitudinal instruction (e.g., "smile," "into the music," "smooth"). Then direct concentration to the take-off for the first jump.
	Immediately following a momentary loss of control (e.g., a fall, a shaky landing).	Adjust tension level. Single attitudinal instruction ("smile"). Note: avoid any thought that reminds you of outcome or that demands perfect performance (e.g., "no more mistakes"). Simply

TABLE A.1 (cont.)

		remind self of what you need to do for the next jump and focus on the take-off.
Football	Immediately prior to the snap from center.	Make needed tension adjustments, remind self of one key to performance, direct attention to the count.
	On defense, just as the quarterback steps up to the center.	Adjust tension, remind self of performance key, direct attention to the count.
	When running a pass route, just prior to making a cut.	Mentally check upper body tension, remind self to relax, talk ball into your hands, eyes on ball.
	On a punt (as the punter just prior to the snap).	Relax tension in upper body, remind self of a single task-relevant cue or thought (e.g., "smooth," "follow through"), direct attention to the snap.
Golf	Immediately after you have mentally rehearsed a shot, at the point you address the ball.	Adjust tension in upper body, especially shoulders. Relax tension in legs on exhale and remind self of a single task-relevant cue (e.g., "firm stroke," "easy backswing"). Eye on the ball.
Gymnastics	Immediately prior to the initiation of a routine.	Adjust tension in neck and shoulders, feel solid contact with ground on exhale. Give self a single tactical or technical instruction, direct attention to the take-off position, mount, etc.
	In floor exercise, immediately prior to the initiation of a tumbling run.	Brief tension adjustment, cleansing breath, think of a single task-relevant cue or self-instruction. Direct attention to the take-off point for the first trick.
	On beam, after completion of a trick, when there is a natural pause where a	Quickly adjust tension level and breathing. Give self a single task-relevant instruc-

TABLE A.1 (cont.)

	position is briefly held.	tion, direct attention to setting up the next move.
Hockey	Just as you begin to skate out on the ice for your shift.	Relax tension in upper body, on exhale feel solid on the ice. Give self a single tactical or technical instruction, direct attention to getting into position.
	Immediately prior to a face-off, just before you skate into position.	Adjust tension levels, check breathing, direct attention to controlling the puck.
	Any time you find yourself with a negative, self-defeating thought.	Adjust tension, give self-positive emotional suggestion, redirect attention to gaining control over your part of the game.
Judo	As you assume a ready position just prior to the start (e.g., while grabbing each other's gi).	Adjust tension level, briefly remind yourself of a single positive emotional thought, direct concentration to feeling the movements of your opponent.
	During any momentary lull in the action, (e.g., when a hold causes a major or unexpected change, when you are stalemated or in control).	Use centering to adjust tension level, direct attention toward analysis of situation, then toward preparing for offensive. Center again, and at the end of breath, direct attention to single most task-relevant cue ("focus ki").
Karate	While sparring, just before an offensive move. At this time you are at a distance able to control enough to allow quick internal focus.	Rapid adjustment of tension level, relaxation of muscles in neck, shoulders, and legs. Immediate redirection of attention to the cue that will signal you to attack (e.g., the position of your opponent or the response to a feint).
	Just prior to the start of a contest.	Quick check of tension level. Remind self of one important attitudinal instruction (e.g., "strong," "cat like"). Direct focus on opponent and/or the initiation of an attack.

TABLE A.1 (cont.)

Motocross	Immediately prior to the start of a race. Just before the gate or barrier is dropped.	Check tension levels, especially in chest, neck, and shoulders. Focus concentration to the point on the course to which you want to accelerate.
	Immediately before making an attempt to pass another racer, or before attempting to negotiate a difficult part of the course.	Quickly adjust tension levels especially in upper body since excessive tension will make you unstable on the bike. Remind yourself of the key to success. Attend to the most task-relevant cue (e.g., position of the bike you will pass). Time your move to coincide with the finish of the exhale of your centering breath.
	Immediately after some unexpected event (e.g., a near fall, being passed, etc.).	Quick tension adjustment, mental reminder of something tactical or technical to attend to and redirect concentration to the race.
Shooting	Immediately prior to squeezing off a round in three-position rifle shooting.	Tension adjustment, technical reminder (e.g., squeeze), attention on the sight picture.
	Immediately prior to calling for the target in skeet and trap.	Tension adjustment, tactical or technical reminder, attention directed to point where you expect to pick up the target. Calling for target should be right at the end of the exhale.
	In response to a negative attitude of self-doubt that may occur following a bad shot.	Tension is adjusted, then attention is focused on positive self-talk. In this instance use centering as reminder to give self a needed pep talk.
Soccer	Just prior to the kick at the start of a game or following a goal.	Quick mental check and adjustment of tension. Remind self of a single technical or tactical instruction (e.g., "keep eye on ball," stay be-

TABLE A.1 (cont.)

Soccer (cont.)		tween offensive player and the goal," etc.). Redirection of attention to the game.
	On throw-in.	Quick adjustment of tension level. Remind self of the technique (if necessary), shift attention to an assessment focus (broad-external).
	Just prior to taking a penalty kick.	Center twice. First time adjust tension and shift to broad focus to assess goalie position and decide on placement of kick. Second time adjust tension, narrow external focus to kick.
	Just prior to taking a corner kick.	Same as above.
	Just prior to a shot on goal (you are goalie).	Quick adjustment of muscle tension, single technical reminder (e.g., to be up on toes and balanced), narrow-external focus on the attacker. On that part of the attacker that will signal a committed course of action.
Swimming	Immediately prior to the start of a race. Between being called to your mark and getting set.	Adjust tension, single technical instruction (e.g., "good dive," "tight turn," etc.), shift attention to the start. Try to time so exhale is finished as starter says "Set."
	Going into and/or coming out of a turn.	Quick check and adjustment of tension between initiation of the turn and completion of the first stroke. Direct attention toward a technical (e.g., "pull") or attitudinal cue (e.g., "now enjoy the pain, reach for it," "go").
	During the race in response to self-doubt or negative cue or thought	Adjust tension, quick self-instruction (e.g., "stretch it out"), back to race (e.g.,

TABLE A.1 (cont.)

	(e.g., feeling or fear of tightening up).	attend to feeling of pull, etc.)
Tennis	Immediately prior to your serve.	Adjustment of neck and shoulder muscle tension, single technical instruction (e.g., "high toss"), eye on the ball.
	Immediately after a long point, especially if you have lost the point.	Adjust tension, cleansing breath. Single thought designed to be inspirational and positive (e.g., "good point," "stay in there," "this is what tennis is about"). Redirect attention to the ball.
	Immediately after any unsettling experience and/or in response to your own frustration (e.g., after double fault, crowd disturbance, or bad line calls).	Adjust tension, redirect focus to the ball. Time the breath so the end of it coincides with the initiation (either by you or the opponent) of the next point. For example, you would finish the exhale as she/he begins the ball toss for the serve.
Track and Field	Immediately prior to the start of any event (race, throw, jump, vault).	Time the breath in a race so that it is completed as the the starter says "Set." Time the breath in a throw, jump, or vault so it ends as you initiate the activity. In all of these, quickly adjust tension in upper body, shift thoughts to feeling of "being anchored and steady" as you exhale and settle into the blocks or position yourself on the runway or in the ring. Single tactical or technical instruction and then focus concentration on the start or initiation of movement.
	During a race at a predetermined critical point (e.g., the last quarter or	Quick tension adjustment, breathing adjustment. Shift attention quickly to a posi-

TABLE A.1 (cont.)

	when being passed or when doubts begin to surface).	tive self-instruction, redirect attention toward execution (e.g., "lean," "drive," turn-over," etc.).
Volleyball	Immediately prior to the serve.	Quick tension adjustment in neck and shoulders. Single technical reminder. Direct attention to the ball.
	Between points.	Centering is used to control tension, check breathing and speed recovery. Following the breath, concentration is quickly shifted to a broad-external focus to check player positions.
Wrestling	Just prior to the initiation of activity.	Tension adjustment, single self-instruction. Redirection of concentration on to opponent.
	When "stalemated," just prior to attempting a counter or shifting a hold.	Center twice. First time, ad-just tension and shift to an analytical focus to make a plan and prepare to act. Center again, and shift to a narrow-external focus as you initiate your move.

Appendix B

Attentional Requirements for Different Sports

TYPES OF CONCENTRATION

Several different types of concentration were presented through the first few chapters of the book. In chapter 1, the concept of total awareness was introduced; this type of attentional focus allows you to be aware of everything that is going on around you. A much narrower focus of attention or concentration, the "focus of ki" was explained in chapter 3; this type of concentration directs all of your energy into one task or move. In chapter 5, the necessity to analyze and to plan was discussed. During this time you direct your attention internally to recall past information, to anticipate the future, and at the same time, to deal with a great deal of information. Thus, you have a broad-internal focus of attention when you analyze. Finally, in chapter 6, the concept of mental rehearsal was introduced. To systematically rehearse, you must focus attention in a narrow way and direct it internally.

It is important for you to be aware of each of these types of concentration, to be able to see when each is demanded by the competitive situations in which you find yourself. Figure B.1 presents the four different types of attention. As you can see from the figure, each of the attentional styles can be described on the basis of two dimensions: The *width* of the attentional focus, or how much information you try to process at one time, and the *direction*, external or internal, of the focus.

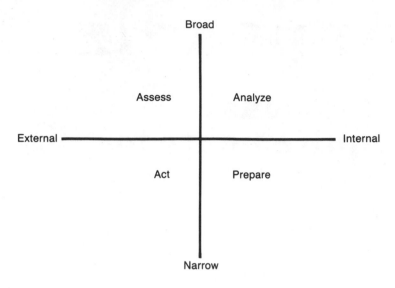

FIGURE B.1 The four different types of attention required in most athletic situations.

The aikido instructor surrounded by several possible attackers illustrates the type of concentration that is required by those sports situations where you must rapidly scan and *assess* what is going on around you. To narrow attention too soon means to fail to see important performance-relevant information. The assessment type of concentration is defined as a *broad-external* focus of attention. You are taking in a great deal of information from the world around you, but are not concentrating on any one bit of information more than any other.

As the assessment process is complete, you either react automatically to what is going on (as a boxer would react without thinking to an opponent's punch), or you momentarily shift attention internally to *analyze* and to plan. This type of concentration occurs when a coach, for example, takes in information from the environment, compares that information with past history (through the use of memory), mentally tries a number of alternatives, and attempts to anticipate the consequences of each. This type of concentration is defined as a *broad-internal* focus. Some sport situations require very little of the athlete in terms of analytical thinking, for everything is automatic; others require a great deal of analysis and assessment.

Once a situation is assessed and analyzed and a game plan has been developed, athletes often find themselves in the position of having to *prepare* to get themselves mentally and physically ready. This involves the third type of concentration, developing a *narrow-internal* focus of attention. In effect, you direct attention internally in order to systematically check and/or rehearse the exact process you are about to experience. The important difference between this type of attention and a broad-internal type of concentration is that no decisions are being made. The game plan is set; now all you are doing is mentally rehearsing the specific steps to overlearn the response.

The final type of concentration is illustrated by Tom Petranoff throwing the javelin (see page 13). This is a very narrow-external focus of attention. Thoughts are directed to the execution of the throw and to nothing else. Tom is not analyzing, he is not rehearsing, and he is not assessing. This is the "focus of ki," the type of concentration that we use to *act.*

The primary goal of my mental training program is to make you aware of the different attentional demands of your sport, and then, as the situation changes, to provide you with the skills necessary to shift fluidly from one type of attention to another. Using Tom as an example, there is a time and place for assessing and analyzing. Tom needs to *assess* his own level of performance and development relative to the competition. Then, he needs to *analyze* in order to develop a training program that will help him accomplish his training and performance goals. Once that is done, he must *prepare*, or rehearse, and he must *act*, or perform. For Tom, the periods for each type of concentration are more distinct than they are for some other athletes.

Common attentional demands for different sports and different positions within sports are outlined below. Table B.1 is concerned only with the demands made on the athlete during competition. For this reason, some of the sports make relatively little demand on the athlete for either *analysis* or for *preparation*. These two internal focuses of attention are, or should be used, in practice and in the development of skill in virtually every sport. Their use during competition, however, is more limited. To help you see how attention must flow and shift from one type of focus to another, the numbers 1, 2, 3, and 4 have been used to indicate the order that a particular type of attention is used. For example, a 1 under "Analyze" would indicate that this is usually the first type of attention required during competition. To further clarify the outlined attentional sequences, a narrative is provided following the Table B.1.

TABLE B.1
Attentional Demands in Sport

SPORT OR POSITION	ASSESS	ANALYZE	PREPARE	ACT
Aikido	1	—	—	2
Archery	1	2	3	4
Auto Racing	1	2	—	3
Badminton				
Serve	1	2	3	4
Point	1	—	—	2
Baseball				
Pitcher	1	2	3	4
Catcher	1	2	—	3
Hitter	1	2	—	3
Fielder	1	2	—	3
Basketball				
Free throw	—	—	1	2
Fast break	1	—	—	2
Time-out	1	2	3	—
Side-out	1	2	—	3
Billiards	1	2	3	4
Boxing				
Sparring-feinting	2	3	4	1
During an exchange	1	—	—	2
Diving	—	—	1	2
Drag Racing	1	2	3	4
Fencing				
Sparring-feinting	1	—	—	2
During an exchange	1	—	—	2
Figure Skating	3	—	1	2
Football				
Quarterback-Linebacker	1	2	—	3
Halfback-Cornerback	1	—	—	2
Pass receiver	3	4	1	2
Lineman	—	—	1	2

TABLE B.1 (cont.)

	1	2	3	4
Golf	1	2	3	4
Gymnastics				
Vault	—	—	1	2
Beam	3	1	1	2
Floor exercise	3	—	1	2
Hockey	1	—	—	2
Judo				
Sparring-feinting	2	3	4	1
During an exchange	1	—	—	2
Karate				
Sparring-feinting	2	3	4	1
During an exchange	1	—	—	2
Motocross				
Race start	1	2	—	3
During the race	1	2	—	3
Shooting				
Skeet and trap	2	—	1	3
3-Position rifle	—	1	2	3
Rapid fire pistol	—	—	1	2
Soccer	1	2	—	3
Swimming				
Sprints	—	—	1	2
Distance	1	2	3	4
Tennis				
Serve	1	2	3	4
Return	1	2	3	4
Point	1	—	—	2
Track and Field				
Sprints	—	—	1	2
Distance	1	2	3	4
Throws	1	2	3	4
Vault	1	2	3	4
Jumps	1	2	3	4
Volleyball				
Serve	1	2	3	4
Point	1	—	—	2
Wrestling				
Sparring-feinting	2	3	4	1
Execution	1	—	—	2

DESCRIPTION OF ATTENTIONAL FLOW, OR SHIFTING

Aikido

Because the aikido expert practices techniques to the point that all movements are automatic, few if any demands are placed on the practitioner to direct attention internally during a series of moves. In practice (to learn) an analytical focus might be required. Likewise, immediately prior to the start of a series of moves, or when demonstrating centering, the expert may develop a narrow-internal focus (prepare). For the most part, however, attention shifts rapidly back and forth between a broad-external focus (assess) and a narrow-external focus (act). Because aikido experts move in response to the other person, reacting rather than initiating, they first assess then react, then reassess, act, and so on.

Archery

Archery, like many closed skill sports where the athlete determines when to initiate a response, provides the opportunity to use all four types of attention. Typically, archers begin by assessing physical conditions and situational factors such as wind, distance, and heaviness of the air that may affect the flight of the arrow. Having gathered information, they will shift to analyze and plan their shot. They will use the information that they have gained, combining it with past experience, their own physical condition, and so forth to determine how to prepare and execute the shot. They will make a decision about how much elevation is required and so on. Next, they will shift to a narrow-internal focus to prepare. They will use this type of focus to monitor and to adjust their own tension level, and to control breathing and the physiological factors that might affect the accuracy of their shot. Finally, they will lock attention onto the target by developing a narrow-external focus, as everything is keyed to the release of the arrow. As soon as this sequence has been completed, assessment will begin again with new information having been gained from the results of the previous shot.

Auto Racing

The sequence listed for auto racing places heavy demands on sensitivity to the environment. The drivers must be aware of race conditions and what is going on around them. They must be prepared to react (narrow-external) instinctively to rapidly changing conditions. During the race there are times for analysis and planning. The idea of a regular repeating sequence (e.g., as is the case with archery) would be difficult to program. Assessment of conditions occurs, and this occasionally may be followed by analysis which is then followed by action. More often than not, the analysis can be left out.

Badminton

You will notice that two different situations have been identified in badminton. In one situation, you have that part of the game that is under the control of one of the players (in the sense that the player dictates when the action will start (the serve); in the other, you have that part of the game that consists of a rapid series of actions and reactions. On the serve, because the server can control the tempo, there is time for assessing the game conditions (e.g., current score, conditions in the gym, position of the other player on the court, etc.). There is also time to analyze this information, taking the external conditions and mentally comparing them to past history (e.g., thinking about strategy in similar situations, reminding yourself of the opponent's strengths and weaknesses, etc.). Then, the athletes can prepare by centering and by adjusting tension levels. Finally, they shift to a narrow-external focus to begin the point.

When the point is actually in progress, there is relatively little time for analysis and/or rehearsal (preparation); instead attention shifts rapidly from a broad focus that allows you to see the position of the other player on the court to a narrow focus (external) as you hit your return. Like the aikido expert during the point, you should be so familiar with strategy given the opponent's position on the court that conscious analysis (in order to plan your return) is not needed.

Baseball

In baseball, the attentional shifts by position are fairly similar except for those of the pitcher. Although it is possible for hitters, catchers, and fielders to develop a narrow-internal focus to center and to adjust tension levels, they are not usually in a position to engage in any extended rehearsal of what they intend to do. In fact, to anticipate what is about to occur may invite disaster. The pitcher, on the other hand, controls the action and, therefore, does have time to mentally rehearse each delivery.

Typical sequences for hitters, catchers, and fielders include assessing the game conditions just prior to each pitch: what is the score, how many outs are there, who is at bat, what is the count, and so on. Next, they analyze the situation, recalling information that they learned about the opposition's strengths and weaknesses. The pitcher, catcher, and fielder all think about the hitters' strengths (e.g., what pitch they hit best, where they hit it) and weaknesses; they think about the opposition's past history (e.g., tendency to bunt, hit and run, steal, etc.) under these conditions; and then they come up with a plan. Finally, they zero in on the most task-relevant cue (e.g., the ball as it is delivered).

Basketball

In basketball, the athlete who is taking a free throw is in a position to dictate the flow of the game, able to take a reasonable amount of time to prepare and to take the shot. Positions at the line and around the key are fixed. The athlete does not have to assess the situation nor is much analysis required. At this time, the only job is to make a basket. Thus, they must prepare, centering to adjust tension levels (preventing excess muscle tension in neck and shoulders from interfering with the shot); then they must narrow attention and focus on the basket.

After the free throw, the ball must be inbounded. The player responsible for throwing in the ball should be capable of rapidly assessing (broad-external) and analyzing the positions of the other players. Then, he or she must be able to narrow in order to make the pass (act). The defensive players' assignment at this time requires more of a narrow-external focus: They attend to the person they are guarding, attempting to determine from movements and expressions what is happening on the rest of the court. Reactions must be instinctive, and there is little time for any extended rehearsal.

On a fast break, the athletes involved are shifting very rapidly from that assessment type of concentration to a narrow focus as they pass, shoot, attempt to intercept, and so on. Very little is required in the way of analysis or preparation. In fact, the direction of attention internally in such a rapidly changing situation is likely to be destructive, no matter how well intended and no matter how positive the attitude and thoughts.

Obviously, time-outs in basketball are taken to regain control in order to analyze and to prepare for the remainder of the game. Often, analysis has been going on during the game, but only by the coach because the players have simply not had the time to think. The time-out lets everyone assess the situation, consider the analysis (offered most often by the coach), prepare by regaining control over arousal and tension, and then shift back to that broad-external focus as the time-out ends and they move back onto the court.

Billiards

As a sport, billiards is much like archery in terms of both attentional demands and the demands for control over muscle tension and coordination. A typical attentional sequence involves assessing the situation, including position of the balls on the table, game score, skill level of the opponent. Then, information is analyzed and a shot is planned. Next, attention is directed internally as the shot is rehearsed and as tension levels are adjusted and breathing controlled. Finally, attention narrows and becomes focused on the point that allows the player to stroke the ball in the desired manner. The athlete's analysis must involve the ability to think several shots ahead.

Boxing

Boxing and most combative sports such as karate, fencing, wrestling, and judo, require at least two different attentional sequences. When the athletes are at a distance testing each other through feints, a typical sequence involves *action* (narrow-external) when a tentative or probing move is executed; then assessing (broadening attention) to see how the opponent reacts (broad-external); then analyzing, using the information gained in combination with past experience to determine a future course of action, for example, to predict how the opponent will react to a certain move; and then preparing to execute the move by quickly mentally rehearsing when and how you will attack. The actual attack now follows requiring a narrow-external focus as all of the energy is directed towards the punch, blow, kick, and so on.

Obviously during an exchange of blows, there is little time for analysis or for any systematic rehearsal of moves. If the boxer's reactions are not automatic, he is in trouble. Thus, attention is shifting very rapidly from a broad focus to a narrow focus, but with the direction always being external.

The experienced fighter will alter this basic format slightly when he gets hurt. At this time, he will have trained himself to cover up and hold in order to give himself time for recovery and to briefly plan and analyze how to survive. One of the ways psychology can help fighters is to teach them to recognize when they need to tie up their opponent.

Diving

As a sport, diving makes very few demands on the athlete for broadening attention. During competition, little is required in the way of either assessment or analysis. Instead, divers must narrow attention to control tension levels and concentration. They control the flow of action, much like the archer or the billiards player. At the time they come to attention on the board or tower, they need to shift their thoughts internally momentarily, and to check and to adjust breathing and muscle tension levels. Then, once they are physiologically prepared, they must direct their concentration toward the single cue that is most relevant to the execution of the particular dive they are attempting. Most often, this will involve attending to some aspect of the take-off, such as their hurdle step, arm swing, and so on.

Drag Racing

A drag racer must perform in several heats or trials which last for a very few seconds. Often, drag racers must engage in assessing race conditions (e.g., condition of the track, of both cars, analyzing the time needed to make it to the next heat, and using a broad-internal type of attention to attempt to anticipate the opponent's speed in order to "dial in" their own speed. Then, they must *prepare* by settling themselves down at the line, mentally going through their own checklist to make sure that they and the car are ready, and then directing attention externally to the timing lights. As they leave the start, in order to control the race they must rapidly shift from continually assessing movement of the car, for example, to acting.

Fencing

As with boxing and other combative sports, a fencer may engage in a great deal of precompetitive analysis and preparation. Viewing films of an opponent provides the opportunity to analyze style and to plan how to counter and attack. Prior to the competition, the athlete can mentally rehearse the anticipated situations and their responses. This stage of preparation requires good analytical ability and the capability to focus in a narrow-internal way.

Once in the competition, two types of attentional sequences tend to occur. First, there is a sequence associated with feeling out the opponent. At this time, the fencers feint a move (requiring a narrow-external type of attention), broaden the external focus and quickly assess the opponent's response, and shift internally to analyze and plan. The information gained as well as previous learning is used to develop a method of attack. Next, the fencers quickly rehearse the situation for which they will be looking. They shift to a broad-external focus as they assess (waiting for the proper moment), and finally they narrow attention ("focus their ki") as they attack or act in response to the anticipated cues.

Once an exchange has been initiated, the response sequence must continue automatically. There is little time for conscious analysis; instead attention remains externally focused and reactions are instinctive. The athletes rapidly shift attention from a broad to a narrow focus but always direct their attention externally.

Figure Skating

The figure skater has some control over the initiation of the program. He or she can signal the start of the music which means he or she has time to mentally prepare and to systematically rehearse the program prior to execution. Ideally, the program does not change; for example, he or she knows the jump sequence, the exact length of time required and so forth.

Once skating begins, the athlete needs to shift from acting (a narrow-external focus) as a jump is initiated to assessing, quickly allowing attention to broaden to bring in information about the landing, and the position on the ice, and so on in order to set up for the next jump. Although analysis should not be required (consciously weighing information to make decisions and choose from several options), the athlete will have time between jumps to shift attention internally in order to prepare. This is done to narrow and to adjust tension levels and breathing, then to direct attention externally to the take-off point for the jump or spin.

Football

Several different positions make different attentional demands in football. A typical sequence for a quarterback and/or linebacker consists of quickly *assessing* the entire field. Next, the athlete shifts internally to analyze, using previous learning to help select an offensive or defensive play. Although there might be time for shifting to a narrow-internal focus to adjust tension levels, there would not be the time to systematically rehearse the actual play during competition. It would make little sense to do this anyway because several options may develop and the athletes would just distract, confuse, and overload themselves by trying to prepare for all of these in a systematic way. Instead, after adjusting tension, they must shift attention externally to execute. The quarterback narrows and focuses on receipt of the ball from the center. The defensive player directs attention to a few "keys." Then, as the play unfolds, the athletes broaden attention again to quickly assess, then narrow as they act, and so on.

Good quarterbacks will be able to assess, adjust tension levels by centering, and narrow as they execute. Often, coaches reduce the responsibility of the athlete to engage in analysis by calling plays from the sidelines.

The positions of quarterback and defensive linebacker can be contrasted to those of offensive halfbacks (running backs) and defensive cornerbacks. Both of these athletes must be capable of rapidly reading the environment and reacting instinctively to critical changes. The dominant attentional focus is external with very little demand, or time for conscious analysis or preparation. This athlete must have a good "street sense" and be able to survive on instincts.

Pass receivers have assigned routes that they must run. This means that they initiate their own movements and react less to the defense. Because they know the route they are supposed to run, they are in control and can actively prepare or rehearse the route. Thus, they might begin a play at the line by preparing (narrow-internal), adjusting tension level, and mentally rehearsing the route. Then, they develop a narrow-external focus at the snap of the ball. Attention remains narrow and externally focused, shifting from the route to the ball as they catch it. Then, having caught the ball, they are in a position to broaden attention in order to assess the position of other players. They must react instinctively to what they see by again narrowing as they begin their run.

The attentional demands placed on interior linemen tend to involve a narrowed attentional focus. For the offense, there is the opportunity to mentally rehearse once the play is called and prior to execution. The offensive lineman knows the play, and the signal allows for an internal focus and some mental practice. The defense must be ready to react to the snap of the ball, to read the actions of the offensive line, and then to react to those actions.

Golf

Like the sport of archery, golf requires all four of the types of attention described in this book. Prior to each shot, the golfers must assess the competitive conditions. They must be aware of a large number of external factors such as position of the ball, distance to the green, conditions of the wind and fairway or green. Next, they must analyze the information that they observe, recalling past shots, club selections, and so on. Once they have decided on a particular club and shot, they must prepare themselves. This will involve centering to adjust tension and concentration and some type of rehearsal of the actual shot. Finally, attention will narrow and become externally focused as the golfer addresses the ball and initiates the swing.

Gymnastics

In gymnastics, all routines, whether they are on beam, bars, vault, or floor, are initiated by the athlete. This means that the opportunity for mental preparation and centering immediately prior to beginning the performance is always possible. The athletes should have a regular mental checklist to go through systematically as they prepare. This would involve rehearsal of the routine itself and adjustment of tension level and concentration.

In an event like the vault, once preparation is complete, all that remains for the gymnast to do is to narrow attention on the point of take-off and then execute. Thus, the only shift required is from a narrow-internal focus, to a narrow-external one. In events like parallel bars, uneven parallel bars, horizontal bars, beam, and floor exercise, there are additional opportunities for assessing, for example, becoming aware of body position on the mat or in the air, and then making automatic adjustments in the routine to compensate for minor and or major errors. In these events, attention begins by being focused in a narrow-internal fashion as the athletes prepare. Then, as the routine begins, they shift attention quickly to a narrow-external focus (e.g., to where they will catch the bar or take off from the floor). During the space between tricks, and at transition points in the routine, there is an opportunity to assess performance by briefly broadening attention to become aware of both external and internal kinesthetic cues that tell the gymnasts whether or not they are on. In reaction to these cues, adjustments are automatically made, and attention narrows and focuses externally for the next catch or take-off. Occasionally, there is enough of a pause built into a routine, such as in a floor exercise after a tumbling run and on the beam, that it is possible for the gymnast to once again direct attention internally, centering to adjust tension levels and to redirect attention.

Hockey

In progress, hockey provides its athletes with little opportunity for analyzing in a conscious, logical fashion, and/or for the systematic rehearsal of a pass, check, or shot. To a great extent, attention must rapidly shift from a broad-external (assess) focus to a narrow-external one (act-execute). Skills must be practiced until they are reflexive. Occasionally when taking the puck behind your own net, there is an opportunity to assess and analyze, setting up a play. Those pauses in the action can also be used to center momentarily in order to check and to adjust tension levels before continuing.

Judo and Karate

Judo and karate are both contact sports in which the athlete must assume both an attack and a defensive position. As with boxing, there are times in a contest when you test an opponent by feinting a move. It is at this time that you learn something about the opposition's defense and counters and about the likelihood that a particular punch, kick, or throw, will work for you. The attentional sequence that is involved consists of a narrow-external focus as you feint. Then, immediately after the move, you broaden attention, still keeping it externally directed so that you will see how your opponent reacts. At this time, you pick up facial as well as body cues. Next, you shift your thoughts to an internal focus as you quickly analyze and select an attack. Just before the actual attack, you prepare by quickly, mentally checking yourself, adjusting tension levels and breathing, and telling yourself for what opening you are watching and on what to focus attention.

During an exchange of punches, or kicks, or when countering an opponent's move, there is no time for conscious thought (analysis) and rehearsal (preparation). At these times, your reactions must be automatic. Thus, in the middle of a flurry of activity, attention would be externally focused and would shift primarily along the width dimension. You would continually jump from assessing and making yourself aware of the environment to acting as you narrow and execute your own technique.

Motocross

The sport of motocross can be extremely demanding attentionally. As with auto racing, during the event, there is little time for the rider or driver to develop a narrow-internal type of attention. Any systematic rehearsal of the course that goes on will usually occur prior to the race.

Because conditions can change so rapidly during a race, the primary attentional demand will be for an external focus, an awareness of the conditions of the course, position of other riders, your own bike, and so on. Any analyzing will have to be conducted at an almost "preattentive" level. As with other sports, decisions such as about when to pass and how to take a turn will have to be made based on information brought in while you are assessing. Analysis will be almost instinctive, based on experience. To illustrate the difference, there are times when athletes are concentrating so hard that they are literally talking to themselves, asking and answering questions at about the same rate of speed as if talking with someone else. At other times, when competitors are highly experienced, the answer pops into mind without having to be verbalized by questions. At these times, what is perceived automatically triggers the desired answer or end output without going through all of the analytical steps. This occurs because these conditions or similar ones have been experienced many times before. It is this ability that allows a good motocross rider to take risks that other riders would not take. The athlete has the ability to shortcut the analysis. With the rider who has developed the ability to shortcut the analysis process, attention shifts during the race from assessing to analysis to acting. One of the characteristics of those riders who seem to hang back is that they spend too much time consciously analyzing and asking "what if" questions. It is this process and self-doubt that keeps them from reacting and taking risks.

Apart from what goes on during the race, the motocross rider has a special challenge at the start. All the bikes are lined up and each tries to be first through the first turn. Being successful at the start involves (a) being the fastest qualifier and getting your choice of position on the starting line; (b) being able to react quickly to the start signal; not anticipating so much that you slam into the barricade, but certainly not sitting back; and (c) knowing exactly how you want to go into the first turn. The start provides the opportunity to center, adjust tension, and direct concentration towards the starter's signal. Attention will shift from a narrow-internal focus (prepare and rehearse) to a narrow-external focus (react to the starter's signal), to a broad-external focus (assess success and position), to a narrow-external focus (act in order to negotiate a turn, recover, pass a rider, etc.).

Shooting

As a competitive sport, shooting requires tremendous control over muscle tension and breathing. Excessive muscle tension and/or hyperventilation can make it all but impossible to react quickly enough to a moving target, or to hold a reasonably steady pattern on a stationary target.

In a moving target sport like trap and skeet, the typical attentional sequence might be as follows: As you step up onto the station, you begin by assessing the conditions. You have noticed wind conditions and how the targets are flying. You analyze this information and use it to help make critical decisions about gun position. Next, you narrow and direct thoughts internally as you adjust tension levels and rehearse the movements you will go through as you react to, track, and destroy the target. Once you are ready, you call for the target. At this point, attention broadens and is externally focused (assess). Once the target is picked up, tracking becomes an automatic response, and for many shooters, attention begins to narrow and to focus exclusively on the target or on their sight picture. There are other shooters, however, especially in skeet, who retain a relatively broad attentional focus. Their sight picture includes a large area in front of and behind the target. These shooters swing through the target and fire; they do not hold a lead.

In a sport like three-position rifle shooting, the athlete has more control over the competitive situation. The stationary position of the target demands a very narrow focus of attention. A typical attentional sequence for the three-position rifle shooters would be to first analyze by recalling where their practice rounds hit the target, what their sight picture was when the round was squeezed off, and what special conditions existed on the range that might affect shooting. Then, after loading the round, they narrow attention and focus internally. At this time, they may begin by rehearsing exactly what they want to see and do. Following the rehearsal, they calm themselves down in a systematic way checking muscle tension and breathing. Then, they narrow attention on the sight picture and act.

In a sport like rapid-fire pistol, there is obviously little time between rounds. An analysis that occurs must be at a preconscious or subconscious level. The shooters may begin by narrowing attention and focusing internally in order to rehearse the shooting sequence and to center and to calm themselves down. They shift to a narrow-external focus in order to fire. This focus is sustained until firing is completed.

Soccer

In many ways soccer is like hockey. Players need to have some sense of what is happening on the entire field, especially if they do not have the ball. A primary attentional demand in soccer is for a broad-external focus of attention. Once they see the position of other players, they must quickly analyze and make appropriate adjustments to their own position on the field. Obviously, the closer the ball gets to them, the less time they will have for analysis. Thus, a fullback might be able to "consciously" analyze and consider several options when the ball is near the other team's goal. As that same fullback is being attacked in his or her own zone, the amount of conscious analysis that can occur is negligible. Ultimately, the focus of attention must narrow and become externally focused as the athlete acts, or reacts, to a shot or pass.

Swimming

Swimming events can be divided into two categories for purposes of an attentional analysis. Short sprints require little in the way of analysis or assessment. The athlete must be ready to react to the starting gun (prepare), and then must act. A sprinter, therefore, can get away with being able to narrow internally and narrow externally.

In longer races there is more time for thought, for making adjustments in stroke, and for strategy to play a role. The longer a race, the more the swimmers will need to be able to monitor their own body conditions and the position of others in the race. This means that several attentional shifts will occur during competition and that the general pattern of shifts will be similar to those found in closed skill sports like golf and billiards. The athletes will broaden and direct attention externally to assess the competitive situation. Then, they will shift to a broad-internal (analytical) focus to make adjustments in strategy. Next, they will narrow their internal focus as they monitor and adjust their own feelings and stroke and as they give themselves instructions designed to direct attention and/or control motivation. Finally, they will shift to a narrow-external focus to concentrate on execution, for example, stroke efficiency and making a turn. Depending on the length of the race, the entire process will begin again, reassessing after the turn, analyzing, adjusting, executing.

Tennis

Tennis, like badminton, has certain times during a game when one of the athletes controls the initiation of activity. Pauses between points provide the athlete with an opportunity to direct attention internally for purposes of analysis and/or preparation. The server should first assess the position of the other player on the court, and analyze by bringing up past information about the opponent's ability to cope with various types of serves, given the position he or she is in. The analysis results in the selection of a strategy. At this point, attention narrows and focuses internally as the server mentally rehearses placement of the serve and the stroke. The same internal focus is used to make adjustments in muscle tension in neck and shoulders that might affect the serve and ball toss. Finally, attention is directed externally to the ball as the point begins.

The player returning serve can go through the same process as the server: assessment of the position of the opponent, and analysis by thinking back on previous games in an attempt to anticipate strategy and placement. Preparation should consist largely of adjusting tension levels. If anticipation becomes obvious, the server will see it and can adjust accordingly. Finally, the player narrows on the ball as the server begins the ball toss.

Although the person returning serve can go through the entire attentional sequence just mentioned, it is at much greater risk than for the server. There is a real danger that this player will still be analyzing when the ball is served, or that anticipation will lead him or her to lean or be out of position. It is preferable for the experienced player to make adjustments automatically without conscious thought and *planned* anticipation.

During the point, the attentional requirements are the same for all of the players on the court. Following execution of your own shot, attention shifts to a relatively broad focus, giving you the information you need to react to your opponent, to narrow your focus as your opponent begins the return.

Track and Field

Track and field is not a single sport, but rather a collection of several different events. Just as these events require different physical types (marathoners do not look like throwers), so they also require different attentional abilities.

Sprinters in track and field, like sprinters in swimming, do not have much time for assessing the field or analyzing competitive conditions. There is time at the beginning of the race for the athletes to narrow and to focus internally in order to mentally rehearse the race, go through their start, and so on. At the same time, they can and should adjust muscle tension levels and concentration. Once this preparation has been completed, attention becomes focused externally in a very narrow way on the starter or on a position on the track. The 9 or 10 seconds that the race lasts provides little opportunity for effectively using systematic shifts in attention. Obviously, some thoughts will occur during a race, but the reactions to these thoughts will have to be automatic and the thoughts themselves are going to be unplanned.

As race distances increase, there is much more time available for strategizing and planning and for making adjustments and corrections during the actual competition. Often, it is very helpful for athletes to go into a race with a planned strategy regarding how they will use their mind and shift attention. Without having some attentional responsibilities your mind is free to wander. Unfortunately, it can wander in directions that will interfere with performance. You will find yourself not attending to important race cues or thinking negative things and tightening up. By training yourself to go through a periodic series of thoughts, you can prevent some of the wandering, or interrupt it before it gets out of control. A typical sequence during a race would include assessing the position of other racers, track conditions, and lap times, analyzing that information by combining it with your own past performance history, your current feelings, the abilities of the other athletes, and making a plan. Then, having made the plan, narrow attention to make any needed adjustments in your own level of tension and your breathing. Narrowing attention and focusing externally to search for the specific cues will allow you to follow your own plan, for example, look for the hill you or someone else will make a break on in a road race; find the person you feel is going to make a break, and get on his or her heels; make a break yourself, surge, and so on.

Throwers, vaulters, and jumpers are all in the position to progress through a natural attentional sequence that involves assessing, analyzing, preparing, and acting because they control the beginning of their own actions. The duration of an attempt or throw is relatively short, and they can take time out between attempts.

The typical sequence for throwers, vaulters, and jumpers starts with assessing the competitive conditions (e.g., how fast is the runway, how slippery is the surface of the ring, where is the wind, what is the approach surface like, etc?). They also analyze adding information about their own readiness for the competition, and the past performances of their opposition. Now they make a decision about how they will proceed, for example, passing the opening height, relaxing and not going all out on the first throw, and so forth. Finally, they narrow and focus internally as they rehearse their attempt in a very systematic way. After rehearsal, they make a last minute check and adjustment of tension levels and breathing, and then shift attention externally to their take-off point or to some other critical cue like that point in the sky where they want the throw to go.

Volleyball

Volleyball, like tennis, is another of those sports that requires two different attentional sequences. When serving, the server and the offensive team, because together they can agree on strategy, have time to assess, to analyze, to prepare, and then to execute. Thus, they can shift through all four of the attentional modes before the point actually begins.

During the point, however, or when on the defensive, there is less time for analysis and preparation. In volleyball, the players must develop an even broader focus to be able to anticipate where teammates and where the other team will be. At the time when the ball comes in your direction you must narrow and execute. Because it is a team sport, team members who are not immediately involved in the play by hitting the ball can do the assessing for the other team members, for example, screaming to let a ball go if it is out, and yelling to let them know their position.

Wrestling

Like the other combative sports, wrestlers do have the opportunity to engage in all four types of attention when they are feinting or faking a particular move. A move is initiated to get the other person to react so that you can assess their ability to respond. To assess, you broaden attention and focus externally. Then, as the opponent reacts, you take the information gained and compare it with what you know about the athlete and various wrestling techniques. Through this analysis, you eventually decide upon a move or technique that you think will work. Next, you mentally prepare by reminding yourself in a systematic way about the conditions that will signal you when to attempt your move. For example, you remind yourself that you are waiting for the opponent to get into a particular position, and to move in a certain way. You make any needed adjustments in your own tension level and then direct attention externally in a narrow way as you watch for the particular cues, or as you start your attack.

When you are on the defensive, or once a series of moves has been initiated, there is little time for analysis or preparation. At this time your attention shifts rapidly from an assessment type of focus to a narrower type of concentration as you react.

Index